WHY JOHNNY CAN'T LEARN

WHY JOHNNY CAN'T LEARN
by Opal Moore

mott media
BOX 236, MILFORD, MI. 48042

All Scriptures are from the King James Version of the Bible.

©1975 by Opal Moore

Printed in the United States of America
Library of Congress Catalog Card Number: 74-27323
International Standard Book Number
  Hard Cover: 0-915134-02-0   Soft Cover: 0-915134-03-9

DEDICATED TO
my sons
and to
all the boys and girls
of America

Prologue

The two-fold purpose of this work is to provide an overview of the direction public education is taking in the United States today and to give those interested in education an understanding of what the "New Education" is all about.

It is primarily directed to: (1) parents — providing them with new insight into what is happening to their school-age children and what can be done about it; (2) teachers — who have withstood adverse pressures but are meeting with more difficulty and those who have unwittingly become part and parcel of "the system"; (3) the Christian community — those dedicated to protecting the faith of children against deceptive teachings in the public schools; (4) members of state and local boards of education — whose decisions affect the lives of forty-five million children who attend public schools each year; (5) legislators — who need to tune out the loud clamor of powerful education lobbies long enough to investigate the root problem of public education today.

What follows are facets of the education that children in today's public schools are receiving.

Acknowledgements

The writer wishes to express her appreciation to:

A.D. Addison, former Publisher of *The News-Review,* Roseburg, Oregon, who granted permission to include in this book, without specific footnoting, certain of the writer's statements which were first printed in *The News-Review;* also to Charles V. Stanton, Editor Emeritus, who edited material frequently submitted by her.

Personnel at the Douglas County Library, Roseburg, Oregon, for their patient and kind assistance in her research.

Rita Spakousky and Ann Stringer who offered many helpful suggestions.

Evelyn Bair who accompanied the writer to dozens of school board meetings.

Jan Claypool who frequently offered encouragement.

Deloris Feak and Mary Thompson whose research on PPBS saved the writer many hours.

Dr. John N. Moore, Professor of Natural Science, Michigan State University, for granting permission to quote at length from his materials.

Rev. R.J. Rushdoony, President of Chalcedon, for his interest and advice.

H. Edward Rowe, President and Editor of *Applied Christianity,* for his suggestions and encouragement.

The Mel Gablers, Educational Research Analysts, for their valued assistance.

The Council for Basic Education for supplying requested documentation.

Those public school personnel of Roseburg, Oregon, who answered questions and made textbooks available for examination.

Friends and acquaintances who assisted in various ways, whose names it is impractical to list.

Her husband and sons, without whose understanding and consideration, the research and writing of this book would not have been possible; and especially to her son, Paul, who proofread the entire manuscript.

Foreword

ROBERT J. HUBER
18TH DISTRICT, MICHIGAN

COMMITTEE ON
EDUCATION AND LABOR

SUBCOMMITTEES:
SPECIAL EDUCATION
GENERAL LABOR

COMMITTEE ON
VETERANS' AFFAIRS

SUBCOMMITTEES:
EDUCATION AND TRAINING
HOSPITALS
HOUSING

Congress of the United States
House of Representatives
Washington, D.C. 20515

December 22, 1974

WASHINGTON OFFICE:
419 CANNON HOUSE OFFICE BUILDING
WASHINGTON, D.C. 20515
PHONE: AREA CODE 202-225-2101

DISTRICT OFFICE:
710 W. ELEVEN MILE ROAD
ROYAL OAK, MICHIGAN 48067
PHONE: AREA CODE 313-399-096

MRS. MARY RICE
DISTRICT OFFICE MANAGER

TO THE THINKING AMERICAN:

I am delighted to have the opportunity of commenting on the book "Why Johnny Can't Learn" by Opal Moore.

The writer quickly comes to grips with the basic flaws in our public educational system. Chapter by chapter each flaw is carefully dissected and analyzed. In this process Mrs. Moore, in clear, logical sequence, demonstrates the fundamental failures of an educational system, which has abandoned the basic teaching precepts and has turned to false, empty promises of untried and unproven theories as a means of improving education.

Our great country is at the crossroads in its approach to public education, and it has been clearly demonstrated that spending the taxpayer's dollars in ever-increasing amounts fails miserably in improving the quality of the educational process.

Today, institutions of higher education are forced to lower standards of admissions, to lower quality of educational textbooks, and lower requirements for degrees, in order to satisfy intellectuals who, in their search for atheistic perfection, have abandoned Christian philosophy, without which there is no education.

I highly recommend that those searching for answers to educational problems study Mrs. Moore's work, which pinpoints our educational failures and offers solutions to correct the abuses before the public educational system destroys itself.

Sincerely,

Robert J. Huber, M.C.

RJH:lp

Introduction

Essentially the conflict in education today is between the concepts of a God-centered and a man-centered universe.

American education was originally committed to a theistic understanding of life. In the course of the past two centuries the secular architects of educational theory and practice have substituted humanistic religion for faith in God. The new religion of man has largely replaced the idea that people are created in the image of God.

The new man of modern education is a product of beneficent evolution. He is a "social animal" who has appeared on the scene as a result of a chance combination of environmental conditions. His confidence is not in God but in the state, whose creature he is. By means of social engineering he hopes to effect a grand millennial reign of man in dedicated service to the all-wise, all-redeeming state. In reality this mind-frame is neither modern nor progressive; it is a throwback to ancient Greek paganism which saw the state as the center of all authority.

The writer of this book stands firm in the conviction that education is a process of discovering and conveying truth, and that truth originates not with man but with God. Education divorced from God, Opal Moore believes, is not education at all but rather a form of indoctrination in the groundless and shifty precepts of humanistic social religion.

A glance over the shoulder at the fascist era and a look at contemporary education in communist lands should suffice to convince every citizen that education as a child of the state, rather than as a servant of God, can easily bring in its wake the bonds of totalitarianism. Let the secular state control the minds of children through "education" and it can program them for its own purposes. Inevitably such purposes will be contrary to the will of God and to the best interests of a people.

Given the departure of American public education from a Christian view of God and man, and given its self-conceived role as architect of a new social order with a deified state at its head, where should Christians stand in relation to the "hot" educational issues which are agitating the country today?

First, Christians must accept a large measure of responsibility for the sad situation prevailing in educational circles. Had we not abandoned the field to the secular educators like John Dewey, who denied even the existence of eternal truths, the appalling developments traced in this book could never have occurred. Evangelical complacency and preoccupation with "spiritual things" gave secularism its opportunity.

Secondly, the current repudiation of the God-centered world view by modern secular education leaves Christians with little alternative but to prefer and lend encouragement to private Christian education. Not to do so is to affirm that the truth of God can better be conveyed by godless agents than by Godly ones.

In the third place, Christians who feel they have a special ministry to perform in the public school will do well to remain in that area of service, making the most of every God-given opportunity to witness for Christ. The wholesale withdrawal of Christians from the public school system is advocated by some with impelling reason. However, it is the position of this book that one of the greatest needs of the hour is for the dynamic involvement of Christians in all areas of educational leadership. Christian teachers, administrators and school board members are desperately needed, not to serve the educational system but to serve God within the system as an enlightening, seasoning, restraining, witnessing element. Opal Moore shows how the Christian may be constructively influential in the educational realm.

"You shall know the truth, and the truth shall make you free," Jesus promised those who decided for Him in a context in which men sought to discredit His person and character. Modern secular education would deny not only His person and character but more especially His self-identification with truth. It is an old story; God declares truth and Satan punctuates it with a question mark. True freedom belongs to those who accept truth from God. Let those of us who love freedom act accordingly — especially in the education of our children.

This trenchant volume by Opal Moore is released to the public at a crucial time in the history of American education. It is "must" reading for every serious educator who believes the Word of God speaks to the educational issues of today.

H. Edward Rowe,
Editor for *Applied Christianity*

Contents

1

ARE YOUR CHILDREN BEING TAUGHT "TO THINK"?

We have left the next generation naked in the face of the twentieth-century thought by which they are surrounded.

. . . Dr. Francis A. Schaeffer
The God Who Is There

"We're teaching children to think," is a popular cliché in public education today. Another is that children are "learning how to learn." All of us want our children to "learn how to learn" and to be able to think clearly. So this sounds very good. We should realize, however, that "clever catchwords can become rallying mottoes, often with very deceptive and misleading results." [1] We need to make certain we understand educators' definitions of their terms.

Traditionally "education" has meant the accumulation of factual knowledge. This included transmitting the cultural heritage from one generation to the next. Education today is assuming a new role and a new meaning. The goal of promoters of the New Education is to cause a change in the behavior of students. The title *change agent* is quite appropriate to this new breed of educator.

How do you change another person's behavior? Thinking controls behavior. So, to change a person's behavior you change his thinking.

In reply to the question "How do you change the thinking of a culture with enormous speed?" [2] two revolutionary professors stated, "Our response is that you do it through the school system. . . ." [3] (These professors, Neil Postman and Charles Weingartner, are coauthors of the recent book, *Teaching As A Subversive Activity*.)

They see "virtually all of our traditional concepts [as] . . . irrelevant. . . . [4] Getting the group to unlearn (to 'forget') the irrelevant concepts as a prior condition to learning" [5] is suggested as "a new

1

educational task." [6]

Included in their list of "out-of-joint" concepts are "the concept of absolute, fixed, unchanging 'truth' . . . . the concept of certainty . . . . the concept that knowledge is 'given,' that it emanates from a higher authority . . . to be accepted without question." [7]

Postman and Weingartner, whose influence in the world of education should not be taken lightly, tell us, "The new education has as its purpose the development of a new kind of person. . . ." [8] They state that economist Robert Theobald "suggested that we have to help the young people in our culture learn a new set of beliefs . . . and a new set of values, which will allow them to live in a totally different world." [9]

If educators are successful in wiping the concepts of absolute truth and certainty and Divine Revelation from the minds of this generation of American children, the next generation will indeed live in "a totally different world." [10]

Would it be permissible in a free society to ask: Who delegated to educators the authority to help the young generation "learn a new set of beliefs . . . and a new set of values" [11] — values and beliefs (in many cases) different from those of their parents?

Is this just a pipe dream in the minds of a couple of revolutionary professors? Let's consider what is happening in countless classrooms across the country.

Subject matter ("facts") to the extent used, is now often treated primarily as substance for imbedding the desired concept or pattern of thinking in the child's mind. This proliferating methodology or pattern of thinking is called *inquiry method*.

"Inquiry's theoretical basis and its practical application best exemplify the total philosophy of the educationists for the 1970's," [12] according to Collin E. Cooper, M.D., who has analyzed the method as it applies to public education. He states:

> Critical thinking, so-called, and forms of inquiry, are used in law schools to examine and learn about areas in the law and their application. The principle of scientific investigation frequently uses the kind of critical thinking about which the layman thinks he knows the definition . . . . seeking alternative explanations and testing them until true and reproducible results are found is a way of life to the good scientist. This is done

by mature minds, in narrow areas of intellectual endeavor. What is being proposed by the inquirists is that such highly sophisticated and very difficult-to-master-and-use techniques be taught to [very young] children. . . . (This is a setting in which so-called critical thinking is foreign and even dangerous to the normal maturation of the child's mind.)[13]

Inquiry method is highly question-oriented, but it is more than question-asking. Rather it is a *process.* The process begins in the first grade in many schools, and in some kindergartens. The objective is to change children's thinking — more precisely, to change the *way* they think.

Other names under which inquiry method travels are: inductive method, Socratic method, scientific inquiry, and discovery. Inquiry may be referred to as a process approach, a conceptual approach, or conceptual inquiry. You may be told, "We're teaching your child to think." Or, "The children are learning how to learn."

Steps in the inductive or inquiry method include: observing, classifying, analyzing, verifying, and inferring — all legitimate in *scientific* endeavors, incidentally.

The *Encyclopaedia Brittanica* mentions that "the ideal of perfect induction has made no impression on practical people, and has proved to be worthless as a guide for scientific people."[14] This means that in many areas it is impossible to test every sample. Unless every sample is tested, you cannot be absolutely certain your answer or conclusion is correct.

"All the important inductions of science are what used to be called imperfect inductions, that is to say, generalizations based on the examination of a bare sample of the whole class under investigation."[15] What is the justification for use of induction — if one cannot be certain his conclusion is correct?

All inductions, and all forecasts based on them, are just more or less sanguine adventures, or speculations. . . . This kind of agnostic solution, if it may be called a solution, is not really satisfactory.[16]

Some inquirists do acknowledge absolute proof and "right" answers in what they call closed systems — such as mathematics.

Induction may have value for experimentation by mature minds in certain areas of advanced study, but what is the justification for induction — described as an agnostic solution — being used as a method of learning, even for six-year-olds, in countless classrooms across America?

In the words of Christian scholar, R.J. Rushdoony, "When men seek to give an atheistic or agnostic interpretation to any fact, it is because they are at war with God and are bent on denying Him."

Fact and Opinion

Beginning in elementary grades in many schools, children are being taught that a statement of fact is a statement that can be proved or verified; and, a statement that can be neither proved nor disproved is a statement of opinion.

A statement that can be verified *is* a statement of fact. That definition of "fact" per se (standing alone without qualification), is only a partial truth, however, and is therefore misleading and deceptive. This kind of "thinking" is erroneous because some "opinions" are facts. For example, if a man, in the year 1000 A.D., had stated, "The earth is round," he would indeed have stated a fact, even though it would not be "verified" through human experience and observation until some 500 years later. His "opinion" would not have become "fact" 500 years later; it already was a fact.

Other factors must be considered. What happens when human observation (or testing by scientific method, to which observation is essential), is accepted as the sole criterion for determining fact (or truth)? How does God fit into such a definition? Can Scripture then be accepted as Divinely inspired? Are vital matters of theological nature relegated to the "opinion" scrap heap? Is all fact or truth limited to the materialist-naturalist realm?

It appears that those who would eliminate God have written their own definition of "fact" (or truth), and have left outside that definition, the greatest Truth of all.

"In this world of utilitarian and materialist values, we seem to have forgotten that truth is not the servant of man. Unless the individual is the servant of truth, both he and his society are doomed."[18] This applies to eternal and Absolute Truth as well as truths of nature and of this world. We meet His conditions for coming "to the knowledge of the truth,"[19] or we remain forever in darkness.

Humanist John Dewey, from whom so many of our educational

fallacies stem, stated, "To generalize the recognition that the true means the verified and means nothing else places upon men the responsibility for surrendering political and moral dogmas, and subjecting to the test of consequences their most cherished prejudices." [20]

The skeptic, like Thomas, says, "Prove it to me or I will not believe." Christ said, "Thomas because thou hast seen me, [observation] thou hast believed: blessed are they that have not seen and yet have believed." [21]

Dewey flatly asserted, "There is no special subject-matter of belief that is sacrosanct." [22] And again: "There is but one sure road of access to truth — the road of patient, cooperative inquiry operating by means of observation, experiment, record and controlled reflection." [23] So, what Dewey was saying is, if "truth" cannot be attained through processes of "scientific inquiry," it cannot be attained at all, and anything attained through any other channel cannot be accepted as truth or fact.

Belief in "scientific method" as the sole road to truth, has become an article of faith for some. It is sometimes called *scientism.*

This is not intended to discredit or belittle the accomplishments of true science. But, as already noted, some realms of truth and reality are outside the reach of scientific "measurement," "observation," "analysis," and "verification."

Genuine Christians find truth accessible through two channels: Knowledge of eternal verities, of absolute and spiritual truths, is attainable through Divine Revelation — the Holy Bible. Knowledge of physical, material, and temporary truths is attainable through use of God-given human intelligence.

This "dualism" distressed Dewey (and still distresses some intellectuals who are influential in today's educational circles). Dewey saw Christianity as divisive and therefore detrimental to the kind of "democracy" he envisioned. The solution, he believed, was to dispense with some of the vital beliefs of historical Christianity. [24] If none of us believed in a Supernatural Creator and all accepted "scientific method" as the The Way to truth and the only way, then all men could share a "common faith." [25]

Should We Sing All Songs To One Tune?

An elementary school principal in 1971, endorsing a particular science program (after naming the various components of "scientific method"), stated it would apply to the "non-scientific" as well as to the "scientific."

Another principal endorsing the same program stated children would "learn to think and act like a scientist." The target, he said, is that "ninety per cent of the children achieve ninety per cent of the objectives." The program, he asserted, will be "basic for the whole United States."

A newspaper account discussing the same science program (referred to as a "process approach"), stated that the program "relates to the teaching of all other subjects in elementary education."[26] I am not judging the quality of the program as a science program. I am trying to point out the scope of "scientific method" in public education today.

Dewey admitted that "scientific method is adverse not only to dogma but to doctrine as well, provided we take 'doctrine' in its usual meaning—a body of definite beliefs that need only to be taught and learned as true."[27] I don't think there's any question as to what Dewey was saying: "Scientific method" is adverse (hostile) to Divine Revelation as embodied in the Scriptures, and therefore to the tenets of Christianity.

Can we permit a methodology which is adverse to Biblical Christianity to relate "to the teaching of all other subjects in elementary education" and to be "basic for the whole United States"?

Now let me emphasize one point: *Christians are not adverse to "scientific method" when it is left in the realm of science where it belongs.* "The Christian faith does not say that no truth can be discovered by reason, or by scientific inquiry, or by pragmatic tests."[28] The Christian faith says that *all* truth cannot be discovered by those means.

To accept as fact or truth only that which can be pressed into the limited confines of "scientific method" makes no more sense than to say the words of all songs must be sung to one tune or they are not really songs. Or, in the words of the Jewish scholar, Will Herberg, "To reduce all meaningful discourse to the scientific is like insisting that all games be played according to the rules of baseball, or else they are not 'real' games at all!"[29]

Furthermore, it is extremely important to understand that "verification" through "scientific method" is not considered as absolute proof. Verification depends upon observation. Observation is considered "relative," and is accepted as evidence, but not as absolute proof.

Where does this leave religious truth? Faith is not measured in a test tube. Man's eternal soul is neither observable nor scientifically verifiable.

Uncertainty carried into the theological realm is called agnosticism.

Truth is synonymous with reality. He who says, "Nothing is factual or true except that which can be observed or verified through methods of science," is actually denying God, the soul, and eternity.

Such a philosophy raises serious questions when taught, (whether explicitly or implicitly), on a wide scale in the public schools attended by children under compulsion of state law and supported by tax dollars.

Supreme Court Justice Arthur J. Goldberg with Mr. Justice John M. Harlan (*Abington* v. *Schempp*) stated the government shall effect "no favoritism among sects or between religion and non-religion," and shall "work deterrence of no religious belief."

Any philosophy taught or promoted in the classroom that denies or plants doubts as to the existence of God—by subtle implication or otherwise—works a deterrence to Christianity. So does any teaching which attacks or undermines the concepts of absolutes or certainty or which (whether through curriculum or methodology) weakens a child's faith in the authenticity of Scripture (as Divine Revelation).

The philosopher, Jacques Maritain, said, "One does not get rid of God by reasoning against Him, but by forgetting Him, by losing sight of Him, by exercising the function of thinking in such a way that the question of God cannot even appear." [30]

John Dewey's corrosive theories live on, inflicting a pernicious blight in countless classrooms.

One Greater Than Socrates

Educators sometimes refer to the inquiry method as Socratic (the possible implication being: you don't know more than Socrates, do you?).

Socrates is credited with being the father of the "inductive method." Science at that time—400 years before Christ—was in its infancy. Socrates was primarily a philosopher, not a scientist. His main concern was with moral philosophy—conduct and ethics. [31]

He believed knowledge and virtue go hand-in-hand: If a person knows what is right, he will do what is right, and happiness will result. [32]

In many cases, this premise is erroneous. The rich young ruler who came to Jesus for advice is a classic example. He claimed to have kept all the commandments from his youth up. When Jesus told him what he could do in order to be perfect, he "went away sorrowful." [33]

It should be noted that Socrates stood against the relativism of the Sophists. The *Encyclopaedia Brittanica* states:

> Thus Socrates becomes, as against the relativism of Protagoras, the founder of the doctrine of an absolute morality based on the conception of a felicity which is the good, not of Athenians or Spartans, or even of Greeks, but of man as man.[34]

Are the contradictions between Socrates' doctrine and the Christian doctrine apparent? Even though Socrates resisted the relativism of the Sophists, his "absolute morality" nonetheless rested on a false foundation — the goodness of man. The Bible teaches — not the goodness of man — but the goodness of God, to fallen, sinful man.

Theologian Emil Brunner, tells us:

> Socratic education evidently has a rationalistic, anti-historical leaning.
>
> It is obvious that Christianity introduced into the world an idea of education which — at first sight — is completely opposed to that of Socrates. . . .Christianity is in itself *paradosis, traditio,* of historical revelation. Something divinely given has to be passed on. . . .[35] The Socratic teacher does not pass on; he does not give, but wants to make the pupil independent of anything given and of any giver.[36]
>
> . . .and this seems to be the sharpest opposite to Socrates — the aim [of Christians] is not the self-active spirit or reason, but the acceptance of something given which is beyond reason. The victory of Christianity, then, seemed to carry with it — in its idea of education — the complete denial of the Socratic idea.[37]

Regardless of what Socrates thought or taught, *One greater than Socrates has since been with us.* It is His Word by which we shall all some day be judged, not Socrates'.

Popular among "inquirists" is the use of open-ended questions to which there are "no right or wrong answers." "Relevance" is the key word. The goal is to encourage "thinking."

Maritain pointed out that Thomas Aquinas "warned teachers . . 'never to dig,' in front of the steps of the student . . . 'a ditch that you fail to fill up.' He knew that to raise clever doubts, to prefer searching to finding, and perpetually to pose problems without ever solving them are the great enemies of education."[38]

Deception

It's unlikely when you raise questions about what is being taught, that any teacher will tell you, "We're teaching your child he cannot be absolutely certain there's a God. God cannot be seen under the microscope or otherwise 'verified'." The teacher will possibly say something like: "We're teaching your child to think. You aren't against thinking, are you?"

Philosophy, if it is to be taught, should be so labelled and studied objectively as philosophy, when the child is mature enough for it. Why should teachers be permitted to teach a deceptive philosophy to children in a captive audience, under the guise of "English" or "Social Studies" or "Modern Problems" or some other harmless-sounding name, while claiming they are teaching children "to think"?

Referring to inquiry method, Dr. Collin Cooper stated, "Of all the systems for inducing a specific classroom environment in which to teach children, this is the most evil."[39]

To live in doubt or uncertainty is to live in perplexity, frustration, confusion. There are many things we can be certain of — absolutely certain. To teach or imply otherwise is sheer deception.

"This aimless uncertainty makes the young a prey to every evil vice.[40] [When] caught in the grip of a world that denies any basic absolutes of truth, they reel to and fro without aim or purpose."[41]

If there is one thing young people need today, it's a plumb line. "A plumb line has a two-fold purpose: positively, it reveals what is straight and true and perpendicular; negatively, and conversely, it exposes that which is crooked and askew and deformed.[42] There is a . . . plumb line, by which we may test all our convictions and conduct, and that plumb line is God's Word."[43]

Does a school system which is forbidden by Supreme Court rulings to offer children the Plumb line as Absolute Truth have the right to chop at it with hatchets guised as methodology? Do educators have the right to promote tenets of a nontheistic, humanistic religion, under the guise of teaching children "to think"?

The theologian, Dr. Francis A. Schaeffer declared, "The *message* of an artist or teacher is to be judged on the basis of truth and the biblical moral absolutes. . . ."[44] Some will say this is "undemocratic" because many students and teachers are non-Christians. That is beside the point.

A teacher whose bread and butter is purchased with tax dollars from the pockets of others has no right to teach anything other than truth.

To teach or imply that nothing is factual or true, except that which can be "verified" by Dewey's narrow definition, indicates spiritual illiteracy or a closed mind or both, and therefore lack of qualification as a teacher.

In the words of Maritain, "It is a sign of childishness to think that a truth ceases to be true because the myopic see it badly or the blind do not see it at all." [45]

The tragedy occurs when the blind are permitted to lead little children.

NOTES

1 L.E. Maxwell, "Perspective," *The Prairie Overcomer,* Vol. 45, No. 10, October, 1972, p. 456.

2 Neil Postman and Charles Weingartner, *Teaching as a Subversive Activity* (New York: Delacorte Press, 1969; seventh printing March, 1970; ©1969 by Neil Postman and Charles Weingartner), p. 212.

3 *Ibid.*

4 *Ibid.,* p. 208.

5 *Ibid.*

6 *Ibid.*

7 *Ibid.,* pp. 216, 217.

8 *Ibid.,* p. 218.

9 *Ibid.,* p. 212.

10 *Ibid.*

11 *Ibid.*

12 Collin E. Cooper, excerpt from remarks delivered to a La Canada, California, Unified School District Review Committee, July 6, 1970 (Appendix One, *The Child Seducers,* by John Steinbacher; Fullerton, California: Educator Publications, Inc., third printing March, 1971), paperback ed., p. 338 (hereafter as Cooper, Appendix One: Steinbacher, *The Child Seducers*).

13 *Ibid.,* pp. 338, 339.

14 *Encyclopaedia Britannica,* 1949, s.v. "Induction."

15 *Ibid.*

16 *Ibid.*

17 Rousas John Rushdoony, *The Mythology of Science,* University Series, Historical Studies (Nutley, New Jersey: Craig Press, 1967; second printing September, 1968), p. 48.

18 George Charles Roche III, *Education in America* (Irvington-on-Hudson, New York: Foundation for Economic Education, Inc., 1969), p. 136.

19 II Tim. 3:7b.

20 John Dewey, *Reconstruction in Philosophy*, Enlarged Ed., paperback (Boston: Beacon Press, sixth printing, August, 1963; First Beacon Paperback edition published in 1957. Original edition, ©1920 by Henry Holt and Co.; Enlarged edition, ©1948 by Beacon Press), p. 160.

21 John 20:29.

22 John Dewey, *A Common Faith*, The Terry Lectures (New Haven: Yale University Press, 1934), p. 39 (hereafter cited as Dewey, *A Common Faith*).

23 *Ibid.*, p. 32.

24 *Ibid.*, p. 84.

25 *Ibid.*, p. 87.

26 "AAAS Installed," *Roseburg* (Ore.) *News-Review*, August 3, 1972.

27 Dewey, *A Common Faith*, p. 39.

28 Ruby Lornell, *We Live by Faith*, (Philadelphia: Muhlenberg Press, 1955), p. 11.

29 Will Herberg, "Modern Man In A Metaphysical Wasteland," *The Intercollegiate Review*, Vol. 5, No. 2, Winter, 1968-69, p. 82.

30 Jacques Maritain, *Moral Philosophy* (New York: Charles Scribner's Sons, 1964; French language edition ©1960 Librairie Gallimard; published simultaneously in United States and Canada), p. 307 (hereafter cited as Maritain, *Moral Philosophy*).

31 *Encyclopaedia Britannica*, 1949, s.v. "Socrates."

32 *Ibid.*

33 Matt. 19:16-22; Luke 18: 18-23.

34 *Encyclopaedia Brittanica*, 1949, s.v. "Socrates."

35 Emil Brunner, *Christianity and Civilisation*, Vol. II, Gifford Lectures delivered at the University of St. Andrews, 1948 (New York: Charles Scribner's Sons, 1949), p. 44.

36 *Ibid.*, p. 43.

37 *Ibid.*, p. 44. Brunner believes we need a philosophy of education (based on the idea that man's personality is rooted in his relation to God) that combines the "Socratic element of self-development with the Christian concept of divine grace." (*Ibid.*, p. 55.) Such an idea for public education, even if acceptable to Christians, would probably not be acceptable to Humanists.

38 Jacques Maritain, *Education at the Crossroads*, The Terry Lectures (New Haven: Yale University Press, 1943), p. 50.

39 Cooper, Appendix One: Steinbacher, *The Child Seducers*, p. 338.

40 "Mother and Dad's Answer," pamphlet (Christian Faith Church, Port-

land, Oregon), n.d.

41 *Ibid.*

42 "No Other Standard," *The Prairie Overcomer,* Vol. 45, No. 10, October, 1972, p. 468.

43 *Ibid.*

44 Francis A. Schaeffer, *The God Who Is There,* paperback ed., ©1968 (3rd American Printing, Downers Grove, Ill.: Inter-Varsity Press, December, 1969, with permission from Hodder and Stoughton Limited, England), p. 161.

45 Maritain, *Moral Philosophy,* p. 288.

2

THE UNCERTAIN WORLD OF THE GRAY THINKERS

Nothing has so shaken our security these days as the philosophy of relativism — the theory that holds ultimate truth to be a mirage, that today's moralities may be tomorrow's joke, that no values are fixed. Against that fluid and spineless philosophy, the Bible stands majestically with its absolutes, not subject to prevailing fashions or circumstances — true yesterday, today and forever.

. . . Rev. Billy Graham
Reader's Digest, May, 1969

What will be the result of learning through inquiry? A special feature article entitled "Teaching and Learning Through Inquiry," which appeared in the May, 1969, *Today's Education* (the Journal of the National Education Association) gives this answer:

> For the students, the most important result of learning through inquiry is a change in attitudes toward knowledge. As they engage in the dialogue of inquiry, they begin to view knowledge as tentative rather than absolute, and they consider all knowledge claims as being subject to continuous revision and confirmation. As they try to provide their own answers to difficult questions about man and his environment, they begin to understand the complexity of verifying knowledge and the processes involved in it. [1]

> As they present their ideas, which are continuously challenged by their peers, students begin to see that value judgments cannot be accepted solely on faith. They realize that judgments about the worthiness of a social action, a group project, or personal conduct stand or fall on the basis of the explicit grounds that support them. [2]

Because the genuine Christian accepts the Holy Bible as the authoritative, unchanging, inerrant, inspired Word of God, the foregoing thesis is in direct contradition to the Christian perspective which declares:

> The Scripture revelation . . . must be the plumb line of our
> actions, and the guiding star of our lives . . . . every circum-
> stance of our lives finds its interpretation there. [3]

Value judgments include moral judgments. When moral judgments
and personal conduct are decided on the basis of the particular situation
and the persons involved, rather than according to God's Laws, we have
man-made morality — situation ethics.

The death of the absolutes (the Ultimate Absolute is God) results in
the philosophy of relativism or "gray thinking."

Thesis is a stand or position on an issue; *antithesis* is the opposite
position or viewpoint. *Synthesis* is the merging of the two opposite
positions. Synthesis is blending or compromise. Relativism is the
synthesis.

The Bible is a book of absolutes. Christ's instructions were absolute:
"Be ye therefore perfect, even as your Father which is in heaven is
perfect." [4] "How could a perfect God say, 'Just sin a little bit'? This
would be impossible. [5] The Christian view is that when a person casts
himself on Jesus Christ as Saviour, at that moment he has passed from
death to life. . . ." [6] He has passed from darkness to marvelous light. "It
means to be acquitted from true guilt and no longer be condemned. This
is an absolute personal antithesis." [7]

The moral relativist says, "My decision and conduct will depend upon
the particular situation and circumstances." (He acknowledges no
Absolute Standard. What is "right" depends upon the situation.)

The Christian says, "I will do what is right in *every* situation in spite of
the circumstances." (What is "right" for him is that which lines up with
Scripture. God's Word as revealed in Scripture is his Absolute
Standard.)

The song, "Shades of Gray," popular in the early seventies, "is a
frightening commentary on a society which has effectively washed the
Creator God out of its conscience. In the absence of the authority of God
every man considers his moral and ethical values as good as the next
man's. When there is no longer a generally accepted voice of authority
many contradictory voices, each claiming to be right breed confusion
and instability." [8]

Confusion and instability abound.

Christ said the foolish man built his house upon sand; the wise man built his house upon a rock.

Sand is loose, yielding, easily manipulated.

A rock is unyielding, firm, inflexible.

How does this apply to public education? What are some of the current catchwords and goals in public education? Flexibility. Tentativeness. Open-endedness. Appropriateness. Relativity.

Those who build upon the shifting sands of relativism are easily "tossed to and fro, and carried about with every wind of doctrine," [9] having no solid foundation, no Anchor. The New Testament declares, "A double-minded man is unstable in all his ways." [10] For him there is no black or white — only shades of gray.

Some argue that the Bible was written by men, that men make mistakes; therefore, the Bible is unreliable. Those who make that charge display either intentional or unintentional spiritual blindness. Man was the mere scribe; the Text was given through Divine revelation and inspiration. [11]

The Ten Commandments are Absolutes. Moses was not the author of these Absolutes; God was. The testimony of God's instructions was engraved "with the finger of God" — not in the sand — but on tables of stone, signifying permanence. [12] The truths of God's Word are *certain, absolute,* and *unchanging.*

Man has the choice of living in accordance with God's Word or defying it. To deny the existence of Permanent Truth and Certainty is to deny the validity of Scripture.

For a school system to undercut the concepts of Certainty and Absolute Truth is to strike at the very roots of the Christian child's faith. Using "inquiry," with its resultant relativist philosophy, under the guise of teaching children "to think," is an insidious attack upon Biblical Christianity.

What happens in homes where parents believe in Absolute Truth and absolute standards of morality, and the child, through indoctrination in the classroom, soaks up the dogma of relativism? Does this help explain the so-called generation gap? Are schools not indeed contributing to that gap?

What about the "mental health" of a sensitive child who is taught relativism at school and belief in Absolute Truth at home — thereby being pulled in two directions?

What happens when a large segment of society rejects belief in Absolute Truth and embraces moral relativism? Will moral decadence result? Are public schools contributing to moral decadence? To delinquency?

Without an outside reference point (the Creator-God), what is the basis for morality? For law? For authority? Can there be any hope for continuing individual freedom and dignity unless man's laws and morals are based upon an Absolute?

Professor Russell Kirk, lecturer and author, described the danger this way: "Unable to affirm or deny anything, they [students] fall prey to any scoundrel who retains some will. Thus Dewey's 'education for democracy' slides toward education for tyranny." [13]

In his album, "Universities Against Truth," Warren H. Carroll Ph.D., declares:

The denial of truth is the basis for indoctrination in the American university today because to deny that truth can be known is to destroy the very cornerstone of independent, individual judgment, leaving the student who has accepted that teaching utterly at the mercy of those who would put a self-serving academic consensus in the place of the truth they have denied. . . . [14]

If this is true at the university level, are not children at the high school and elementary levels even more vulnerable?

Is it possible that teachers who boast they are teaching children "to think" (through use of inquiry method), are themselves incapable of genuine thinking? Have they examined the presuppositions and logical conclusions of the inquiry method with its resultant relativist philosophy? Or are they using this methodology deliberately with full knowledge of its anti-Christian implications? Are some teachers so completely calloused to the rights of others, that they will take advantage of their unique position and dogmatically attempt to undermine beliefs of Christian children, in utter disregard of the Constitutional rights of such children and their parents?

Without absolute answers in academic learning, both the purpose and justification for public schools collapse. If no knowledge is certain, then the whole endeavor of public education is a mockery and an exercise in futility.

If, on the other hand, there are right answers, certain answers, and absolute truth, what is the reason for widespread use of inquiry method with its uncertain (and at best only tentative) answers in the public education system, particularly in areas where certain, knowable answers are attainable? Perhaps the answer can be found in these statements by Maritain:

"If no knowledge is absolutely true it is because there is no absolute in the unconditional sense. . . . [15] If relativity as the only absolute principle has such a fundamental importance it is because this principle delivers us absolutely from God. What miracles of grand surgery!" [16]

NOTES

1 Byron G. Massialas, et al., "Inquiry," *Today's Education — NEA Journal*, Vol. 58, No. 5, May, 1969, p. 41.

2 *Ibid.*, p. 42.

3 Sister Eva of Friedenshort, quoted in "No Other Standard," *The Prairie Overcomer*, Vol. 45, No. 10, October, 1972, p. 466.

4 Matt. 5:48.

5 Francis A. Schaeffer, *The God Who Is There*, paperback ed., ©1968 (Third American printing, Downers Grove, Ill.: Inter-Varsity Press, December, 1969, with permission from Hodder and Stoughton Limited, England), p. 155.

6 *Ibid.*, p. 102.

7 *Ibid.*

8 W.F. Elgin, "The Beginning of Wisdom," *Roseburg* (Ore.) *News-Review*, May 8, 1971.

9 Eph. 4:14b.

10 James 1:8.

11 See II Tim. 3:16, II Peter 1:20, 21.

12 See Exodus 24:12, 31:18, 32:16.

13 Russell Kirk, Foreward to *The Future of Education* by Thomas Molnar, Revised Ed. (New York City: Fleet Academic Editions, Inc., 1970), p. 12.

14 Warren H. Carroll, "Universities Against Truth" (L.P. Album, sponsored by Howard Jarvis; Technical Direction Stereomasters; Hollywood, California: Stellar Records; ©1966, UAT 2002, side 1).

15 Jacques Maritain, *Moral Philosophy* (New York City: Charles Scribner's Sons; published simultaneously in the U.S.A. and Canada — © under the Berne

Convention; ©1964 by author; French language edition ©1960, Librairie Gallimard), p. 285.

16 *Ibid.*, p. 286

3

LOOK WHO'S WIDENING THE GENERATION GAP

The present chasm between the generations has been brought about almost entirely by a change in the concept of truth.

. . . Dr. Francis A. Schaeffer
The God Who Is There

The prodigal son described by Christ almost 2,000 years ago would have made a typical fellow traveler with some of today's Now Generation. His father was "affluent." He disliked the work ethic. He didn't want to wait until he was old to get his share. He wanted it *all* and he wanted it *now*. And his generous father doled it out to him. He wanted to travel and have his fun. So he took a trip. And, like many of today's youth, after considerable "riotous living," he found himself living like a pig.

In every generation, some youngsters have rejected their parents' beliefs and some have not. Today's young people are no different. Technology has made no difference in their basic nature or needs. The countless homes where deep rifts do not exist don't make the headlines. The teen-agers we hear about are the rebellious ones.

Each generation has its hair styles, its dance fads, its clothing fads, its music. While these fads often caused temporary antagonism between generations, eventually the teen-agers grew up, married, and usually were reconciled to the older generation. The natural pulling away of teen-agers which occurs in every generation — and should — is normal and cannot be called a generation gap.

A genuine gap, where it does exist, is not an age gap per se. This is evidenced by the fact that there are today many families where the so-called generation gap between parents and teen-agers is non-existent.

Where a wide gap exists between teen-agers and their parents, it is more likely a morals gap than an age gap. What brings about this morals gap in some families?

Dr. Francis Schaeffer explains, "All people, whether they realize it or not, function in the framework of some concept of truth." [1]

Many of those in the "over forty" age group in our country believe in the concept of absolutes. (Many under forty do, also.) This is true of many non-Christians as well as Christians. Many believe in Absolute Truth, and consequently in absolute right and wrong. This is true whether or not they personally, consistently, abide by that standard.

Some of today's older generation apparently do not understand that many of today's younger generation have embraced an entirely different concept of truth — namely, relativism. To the relativist, God's standards mean nothing.

A genuine gap may exist, then, between those parents who believe in an absolute standard of morality and their children who have soaked up the philosophy of relativism.

Some teen-agers can truthfully throw the "hypocrisy" charge at their parents. These teen-agers, however, do not seem to understand that loving parents, seeing their own mistakes, hope to spare their children the heartache or enslavement they have experienced.

So the line of communication is broken. The parent speaks one language, the teen-ager another. They cannot understand one another. If one opinion is as valid as another (as the teen-ager may have been led to believe in the classroom), then the teen-ager may hold his opinions to be as valid as those of his parents.

In contrast, when both parents and teen-agers rely on the concept of Absolute Truth and absolute Bible standards in moral matters, as the criterion, they stand on common ground. This does not mean they will never disagree on a single minor point, but the likelihood of an unbridgeable gap is greatly reduced. Their basis for morality is the same.

There may be cases, too, where parents and teen-agers both accept relativist morality in which no unbridgeable gap is apparent. For, if anything goes, then no one will object to anything. However, even in these cases, it is likely that deep quarrels may arise over degrees of indulgence by either parents or children.

And I hasten to add there are young people who have accepted the Christ of Absolutes who are putting their wayward, relativist parents to shame.

The erosion of morals among today's youth who are on the far side of the chasm has been the result of numerous contributing factors, and various combinations of these factors. Such as: Mobility. Availability of drugs. Influence of the mass media. The pull of the herd. Rock music. Affluence. Excessive free time. And then there is the blight of "experts" ranging from pediatricians to psychiatrists and psychologists to anthropologists and sociologists to Supreme Court Justices to confused "theologians," some of whom have worsened the problem.

Nor can we accurately analyze the genuine generation gap without considering the contributions the public schools make to that gap.

Such factors as the pull of the herd and the availability of drugs are not themselves the cause of the generation gap. Why do some resist the pull while others do not?

Those "flexible" children whose decisions ("value judgments") spring from relativism are far more likely to bend than those "rigid" ones whose decisions stem from "dogmatic" belief in Biblical morality, or Absolute Truth.

"Flexible" means "easily bent, easily persuaded or influenced." [2] A child whose faith is well-grounded in absolute Bible standards of morality is *not* easily bent, nor does he yield easily in areas involving violation of his religious beliefs.

The great emphasis on "flexibility" in public education today shows itself tangibly in everything from replacing "stationary" walls with "flexible" (movable) partitions — to replacing "rigid" fastened-down desks with loose chairs — to "flexible scheduling." Some educational writings indicate the purpose of certain environmental arrangements is to help induce change in behavior of both teachers and students. The new "humane" classroom environment is designed to help induce "flexibility" in children.

The greater danger lies, however, in the "New Education" curriculum and methodology.

Can anyone believe that the wedge between two generations is not being driven deliberately?

So, the uniqueness of our situation is not that we have a generation of children unlike any who went before (we don't), or that technology has made a new set of values necessary (it hasn't). The uniqueness of our situation is that our own tax dollars are being spent to implant in the minds of our own children, concepts and beliefs which, in many cases, are in severe contradiction with our own beliefs. Who can estimate the incalculable heartache and irreparable damage that may result?

Some teen-agers who are relativists may not smoke pot. Some may not engage in premarital sex. But remember this: The relativists are the "flexible" ones — the ones most likely to yield when the pressure is on. When the teen-ager has soaked up the "flexible" philosophy of relativism, his roots (if he had any) are torn away. He is adrift.

Does this make it easier to understand the participation of some teen-agers in drug parties, in premarital sex, their sloven dress, femininity (of males) complete with long hair, their obsession with rock music, and, in some cases, with sexual perversion? All of these are but symptoms of the disease. When the "experts" tell us drug use is the symptom of a deeper problem, they are right. The problem is the teen-ager lacks an Anchor, an Absolute basis for his morality. It isn't likely, however, that most of the "experts" will give that answer. Many of them need the Anchor as badly as those they are counseling or treating.

If the teen-ager has rejected the concept of Absolute Truth and lives in a relativist world, if he believes one "opinion" is as valid as another, is it surprising that he sees nothing wrong with smoking pot and sleeping with his pill-taking girl friend?

One might suppose that the junior high age — often a frustrating, awkward, or rebellious time for youngsters — would be the ideal age to drive the wedge between parent and child. Some at this age are vulnerable to those who would chop at their belief in absolutes. But others, in spite of physical frustrations and anxieties, ignore the relativist, gray-think doctrine. They realize it doesn't ring true with what they've been taught at home or at church. It's too late for the relativist missionaries to uproot their "rigid" belief in the absolute standards of Bible morality. Their faith in God is an existent reality; they have an Anchor and refuse, even as young teen-agers, to be shaken.

So now what is happening? Not to be outdone, zealous relativist missionaries, determined to free children "to think," are moving (through methodology and curriculum) into the lower grades to inject their toxin. At this tender age, it is all but impossible for a child to analyze, much less refute, subtle anti-Christian philosophy. A California medical doctor, Joseph P. Bean, who has made a study of public education has warned:

> For the last several years parents have found it difficult if not impossible, to communicate with their teen-age youngsters, chiefly because their children had been reoriented in the classroom. Now parents should expect to find alienation from their elementary school age children as well. [3]

NOTES

1 Francis A. Schaeffer, *The God Who Is There*, paperback ed., © 1968 (Third American printing, Downers Grove, Ill.: Inter-Varsity Press December, 1969, with permission from Hodder and Stoughton Limited, England), p. 143.

2 *Webster's New World Dictionary of the American Language*, Encyclopedic Ed., s.v. "flexible."

3 Joseph P. Bean, M.D., *Public Education: River of Pollution* (Fullerton, California: Educator Publications, n.d.); Text of a public speech made at Glendale, California, announcing Dr. Bean's resignation from the Glendale Board of Education, p. 10.

4

THE IMPORTANCE OF MEMORY

So without memory and the extrapolation which it makes possible man becomes
a kind of waif, without a home to say he is from or to feel he is going to.

... Richard M. Weaver
Visions of Order: The Cultural Crisis of Our Time

"Memory is not education, answers are not knowledge. Certainty and memory are the enemies of thinking. . . ." [1] Those statements appear in the controversial book, *Schools Without Failure,* in a chapter entitled "Thinking Versus Memory." The author is psychiatrist William Glasser.

Without memory we would all be reduced mentally to the level of helpless infants. Perhaps what Glasser meant to say was that the process of memorization is not education, or that remembering is not education. (Glasser regards memory as "a lesser function of the human brain." [2])

I mention Glasser in particular because of his current influence in education. (By December, 1973, Schools Without Failure seminar programs had been conducted in twenty-five states.)

With increased emphasis on "thinking" and "relevance," it has become faddish in some school districts to downgrade memorization and the imparting of factual knowledge for its own value. Should children be expected to remember specific "facts"? To give "right" answers on tests? To remember dates, names, definitions?

What is knowledge? Knowledge is knowing. Can you know a subject without "stored" information (facts) about it? Can you "store" any information (facts) without utilizing your memory?

Answers are evidence of knowledge. If you have knowledge in a given area, you can discuss that subject or answer questions — at least some questions — about it. If you don't have answers, do you really have knowledge? Without knowledge, are you educated? Is education possible without substantial use of memory?

It is true, of course, that many facts and experiences *are* recorded in our memories without deliberate conscious effort on our part. Does that mean we should discard the practice of repetitious study? Is the process of memorization obsolete? Can the multiplication tables, lines of poetry, and important historical facts and dates be etched in the memory by another means? Or should children not be expected to master such things?

Can a person who has little or no knowledge of history be called truly educated? Can one have a thorough knowledge of history without "stored," "inert" facts — various names, dates, and sequences of historical events? Can these be learned without explicit effort? Can one intelligently interpret the meaning and significance of "relevant" current events if he has no knowledge and understanding of historical events? Is history important? Is tradition important?

Emil Brunner has said, "Tradition means continuity. . . . Tradition is, so to speak, cultural memory. . . . In order to pass on what has been, one must know it.[3] Tradition is for men in general what the house of the parents is for the child."[4] Without "stored" facts, can there be "cultural memory"[5]?

Does it really matter whether or not you know the answers on any subject as long as you know where to find them?

Suppose your doctor's memory contained no "stored" facts when you're rushed to the hospital hemorrhaging from a severe laceration. (After all, he can always look it up in his medical books, or rely on "scientific inquiry.")

What would you think of an electrician who had to look up the formulas of electricity each time he did a simple wiring job? His efficiency would be equivalent to that of an amateur. And without memorization of safety procedures, he might find his work rather shocking.

Would you hire a secretary who had never mastered the keyboard of her typewriter through use of her memory? (What's wrong with an "alternative" method — like hunt-and-peck?)

Picture a surveyor who had never bothered to learn (through memory) how to use his equipment.

Granted, no one can know everything — even in his own field of work;

all of us at times have to rely on reference books and props of various kinds. It is important that children be taught how to look things up — how to do research. However, failure to make good use of our memories could make us slaves to reference books, slide rules, and other paraphernalia.

It is true that many skills (e.g., typing, performing a tonsillectomy, or laying carpet) can be accomplished with greater speed and efficiency through practice. Even so, the processes must first be set in the memory with conscious, deliberate effort.

How important is memory to "thinking" in the intellectual and academic areas? Is memory an enemy of such thinking?

The late Richard M. Weaver explained the issue with clarity:

> We find that no man has revealed high intelligence in any field of activity without a strong and usually an exceptional memory. . . . [6] In general all intellectuality rests upon our power to associate things not present or only suggested by what is present. Thus the intellectual value of anything depends upon our ability to retrieve it from memory. [7]

> It is therefore impossible to imagine a high-grade or effective intelligence without things supplied by the remembering process. We cannot put two and two together without some work of retention and recall. In the absence of "memory traces," however these may be described, no kind of intellectual activity could be carried on by the individual. It seems beyond question then that any attack upon memory, insofar as this metaphor expresses real facts, is an attack upon mind. [8]

Testimonies of P.O.W.s who survived years of brutal treatment at the hands of Satan's emissaries, the North Vietnamese Communists, speak of the value of memorization. Referring to his fifty-four month ordeal in solitary confinement, Col. Robinson Risner said, "I needed someone so desperately. And the only Person who could reach His hand in was God. . . . I remembered the words of a song we used to sing here at church. . . ." [9] He *remembered.*

P.O.W.s pieced together a living Bible with verses of Scripture they *remembered.* Without memorization there could have been no recall. Some of those verses very possibly had been "stored" in the memories of those men when they were children attending Sunday School, and may have lain "inert" for years. And this living Bible pulled from memory became a prime sustaining power for many of them.

Not only were those who had "stored" Bible verses through the process of memorization able to maintain their own sanity, they were a blessing and help to others. And many of them came back in surprisingly good states of mental health, considering the torturous ordeals through which they had passed.

God, Who created man in His own image, endowed man with memory as a vital, major part of his thinking apparatus. And for a reason. Don't let any educator or psychiatrist tell you otherwise.

NOTES

1 William Glasser, M.D., *Schools Without Failure* (New York, Evanston, and London: Harper & Row, Publishers; ©1969 by William Glasser), p. 38.

2 *Ibid.*, p. 35.

3 Emil Brunner, *Christianity and Civilisation*, Volume II; Gifford Lectures delivered at The University of St. Andrews, 1948 (New York: Charles Scribner's Sons, 1949), p. 30.

4 *Ibid.*, p. 33.

5 *Ibid.*, p. 30.

6 Richard M. Weaver, *Visions of Order: The Cultural Crisis of Our Time*, paperback ed. (Baton Rouge: Louisiana State University Press, 1964; manufactured in the United States by Vail-Ballou Press, Inc., Binghamton, N.Y.), p. 42.

7 *Ibid.*, p. 43.

8 *Ibid.*

9 Col. Robinson Risner, "Seven and a Half Years a POW; Risner: 'God Answered Prayer,' " *Christian Crusade Weekly*, Vol. 13, No. 24, April 22, 1973, p. 4.

5

QUACK-PSYCHOLOGISTS IN THE CLASSROOM

There is nothing new about attempts to control another person's behavior. Physical force has been used since just after man appeared on earth. However, the techniques of warfare more recently developed have led to the invention of new weapons which relegate nuclear explosives to the category of the bow and arrow . . . . When you consider that the ultimate goal of warfare is the control of the behavior of the vanquished by the victor, we are therefore, in the greatest conflict in the history of mankind. Welcome to World War III.

. . . Joseph P. Bean, M.D.
Public Education: River of Pollution

Sixty Million Schizophrenics

A scientist with the National Institute of Mental Health, Dr. David Rosenthal, declared in 1972 there may be more than sixty million schizophrenics in the United States.[1] When you add the neurotics and others with emotional disorders, the total is "almost impossible to estimate. It should be clear that almost no family in the nation is entirely free of mental disorders,"[2] Rosenthal was quoted as asserting.

When I read those allegations, a line from *Brainwashing: A Synthesis of the Russian Textbook on Psychopolitics* ran across my mind: "Propaganda should continue and stress the rising incidence of insanity in a country.[3] Great remarks must be made of 'the pace of modern living' and other myths as the cause of the increased neurosis. . . ."[4] Operatives were advised, "The entire field of human behaviour . . . can, at length, be broadened into abnormal behaviour."[5]

Psychopolitics is defined as "the art and science of asserting and maintaining dominion over the thoughts and loyalties of individuals, officers, bureaus, and masses, and the effecting of the conquest of enemy nations through 'mental healing' " [6]

Many intelligent people will discount Rosenthal's estimate as a wild exaggeration. However, we must keep in mind, as Rushdoony has pointed out: "More than once in history, men have assumed a problem and then provided an 'inescapable' answer." [7]

What "remedy" would Rosenthal and his colleagues propose for possibly "more than sixty million schizophrenics" [8] ? If Rosenthal is correct that "almost no family in the nation is entirely free of mental disorders," [9] what "treatment" would he suggest? Group therapy sessions for every family in the nation? And what preventive for the next generation?

How do the "experts" define the term "mental illness"? How do they define "schizophrenia"?

Even psychiatrists and trained mental hospital personnel cannot be trusted to tell the difference between the sane and the insane. [10]

As a test, eight sane investigators, including "three psychologists, a pediatrician, [and] a psychiatrist," had themselves admitted to mental hospitals in five states. [11]

Real patients in the mental hospitals, in some cases, recognized the pseudopatients as such. But the hospital staffs didn't catch on. [12]

All of those participating in the experiment took notes extensively Some of the real patients were suspicious. Certain staff personnel, however, saw the note-taking as an indication of the mental illness of the "patient." [13]

Following the experiment, one of the participants (a psychologist and university professor), stated, "It is clear that we cannot distinguish the sane from the insane in psychiatric hospitals. [14] The facts of the matter are that we have known for a long time that diagnoses are often not useful or reliable, but we have nevertheless continued to use them." [15]

If the sane cannot be distinguished from the insane in mental hospitals by trained personnel, can they be distinguished outside a clinical facility?

What about the validity of psychological tests used on children at school? Is the potential for damage from incorrect diagnosis and subsequent "treatment" not obvious?

What is "mental health"?

Dr. Kenneth Goff said a group of psychiatrists called on him several years ago to discuss a book he was circulating. Dr. Goff told them he would enter into the discussion if they would first give him a real definition "of what, in their minds, constituted a sane man. After two hours of fighting among themselves," he said, "they were unable to produce an answer." [16]

Living in a dream world, or being unable to differentiate illusion from reality, is considered symptomatic of mental illness. Freud, founder of psychoanalysis, considered all religious doctrines illusions.

Today's agnostic or atheistic psychiatrist or psychologist, who refuses to acknowledge the existence of an Omnipotent Creator-God, may likewise view the person with faith in God as believing a myth, caught up in an illusory dream — like the child who believes in fairies and Santa Claus.

Are those who believe in the Creator-God among the estimated one-in-four American "schizophrenics" who presumably need "treatment"?

There are those who would like to see belief in God made synonymous with "mental illness," if not insanity. One criterion of mental health, to some, would mean freedom from belief in God — Whom they consider to be a myth — an invention of the mind of man.

The irony of this is that the gullible psychiatrist or psychologist who has swallowed the capsule as concocted by Darwin, and who in his headiness, or through ignorance or spiritual blindness, scorns the idea of the Creator-God, is himself, failing to face up to Reality, and is living in illusion.

One well-known psychotherapist, Albert Ellis, Ph.D., (who has called himself an atheist) sees "virtually all the commonly accepted goals of emotional health [as] antithetical [opposite] to a truly religious viewpoint. . . ." [17] He further states:

> Religious moralism patently produces or abets enormous amounts of severe emotional disturbance. . . . Conventional religion is, on many counts, directly opposed to the main goals of emotional health. . . Religiosity, in my estimation, is another name for narrow-mindedness, emotional disturbance, or neurosis. Or, in some extreme cases, psychosis! [18]

Psychiatrist Brock Chisholm, the first director of the United Nations

World Health Organization, expressed this view:

> What basic psychological distortion can be found in every civilization of which we know anything?. . . There is — just one . . . . morality, the concept of right and wrong. . . . For many generations we have bowed our necks to the yoke of the conviction of sin. . . . The fact is that most psychiatrists and psychologists . . . have escaped from these moral chains and are able to observe and think freely. Most of the patients they have treated successfully have done the same. . . .[19]

If Chisholm's statement is true, can we not then assume that most psychiatrists and psychologists have also rejected belief in the Source of "moral chains," leaving them either atheists or agnostics?

The profession of psychiatry has another interesting distinction: the highest suicide rate of any professional group — about six times that of our national rate. Various "explanations" have been offered for this embarrassing statistic among the "authorities" of "mental health."

Some of them, it is thought, may be unable to bear the painful exposure of their own personalities as revealed while undergoing psychoanalysis during their training. (If a psychiatrist-in-training, supposedly normal, cannot bear the ordeal of psychoanalysis, if it is so potentially destructive that it may be a contributing factor to his own later suicide, what is the justification for using it on the mentally ill?)

Another "explanation" is that possibly some enter the field because they have a fascination with the morbid.[20]

Still others, it is believed, study psychiatry in a search for solutions to their own problems and conflicts.[21]

Are those who have escaped "moral chains" qualified to understand even the fundamental, basic meaning of genuine mental health? To formulate or administer psychological tests to children? To diagnosis children's "emotional problems"? To prescribe "treatment"?

Is the hidden objective of improving children's "mental health" in the public school, to set them free of "moral chains" of Christianity? Is the current deluge of anti-Christian relativist propaganda in public education strictly coincidental? Is the current attack on the concept of certainty unrelated?

What are some of the evidences of genuine mental health? Cheerfulness. Serenity. Love, Patience. Contentment. Confidence. Optimism.

And what does Christianity offer? All of these. "For God hath not given us the spirit of fear; but of power, and of love, and of a sound mind." [22] That is mental health.

How many psychiatrists would declare a person emotionally unstable or mentally ill who kneels in a Bible-believing church and sheds tears of gratitude when a load of true moral guilt is lifted?

And how many of these same psychiatrists would ask their clients to take part in "group therapy" sessions where participants are encouraged to be completely "honest" with one another? Where they may shout angrily, embrace fondly, cry hysterically, or confess their ugly, sinful deeds to one another?

Is "group therapy" a counterfeit religion? A confessional before men instead of God? A means by which the participant may have his guilt *feeling* assuaged while the actual moral guilt remains intact, unforgiven by God? Is the sin-cancer being anesthetized?

May the day soon dawn when both group therapy and psychoanalysis will be held in as high esteem as the bloodletting of two centuries ago is held today.

Secular modern man is rootless, without an Anchor. Sinking in the quicksands of relativism, he may grasp for the flimsy straw of hope some humanistic psychiatrist holds out to him. What he really needs is God's touch of mercy and grace.

Unless the psychiatrist or psychologist can point his patient to the Maker of mankind as the Great Problem-Solver and Healer, should his treatment not be considered suspect?

The Bible "unveils the cause of phobias, complexes, psychoses, and neuroses. It will tell you all about yourself — why you act and think like you do . . . . it will reveal the real you. . . . Leave Freud and Jung alone, and see what Jesus and Paul have to say to you." [23]

Is it not sheer folly to consult men for answers about life's frustrations, anxieties and problems who themselves are so blind or arrogant or unwise they refuse to acknowledge even the existence of the Source and Sustainer of all life?

Is it not sheer folly to permit such men to cast their uncertain shadows of influence across our children's intellectual paths behind the walls of the public school?

Sensitivity Training

In 1969 high ranking school officials from some of the major districts in the United States met in a plush motel in Palo Alto, California. It cost the districts represented $2,000 for each administrator present. [24]

Rubbing bald heads together scalp-to-scalp, "touching the skin over a partner's eyes," and backing up to one another on all fours for a little "bottom-bumping" were among activities engaged in. [25]

In Portland, Oregon, in the late sixties, about fifty school officials participated in a sensitivity training session. Their activities included removing shoes, being led with eyes closed by a partner, and falling backwards to be caught by trustworthy colleagues. [26]

Some of the names under which sensitivity training may travel include these:

Group dynamics	Group criticism
Leadership training	Human relations training
Human potential workshop	Group counsel
T-group	Group therapy
Encounter	Rap sessions

New aliases are likely to appear as these names become associated with sensitivity training.

Sensitivity training sessions for teachers may be sold to naïve school boards as "in-service training" or under the guise of "teacher workshops."

A writer in *Educational Leadership*, (the official journal of the Association for Supervision and Curriculum Development, NEA), stated, "Many thousands of school people have experienced sensitivity training." [27] (Sessions they attended were not necessarily school-sponsored or tax-supported.) "Many manage to bootleg training devices into the classroom. . . ." [28] he stated.

Sensitivity training in the classroom may take such forms as:

Maintaining eye-to-eye contact with another person for a certain length of time

One student, with eyes closed, being led by another

Looking at a specified object (such as a blank piece of paper or a doorknob) for a certain length of time

Falling backwards to be caught by others

Sensory awareness exercises (experiences in touching, tasting, listening, or smelling)

Self-awareness exercises (physical: body awareness; emotional
    awareness: anger, love, etc.)

Group consensus games

Simulation games

Role-playing

Non-verbal exercises (communicating without speaking)

Group criticism

It is easy to see how sensitivity training (unidentified as such) can be integrated into the curriculum and used (particularly on young children) without the knowledge or consent of parents.

For example, what does the phrase "communications skills" mean? To have command of one's native language? The ability to read, write, and speak fluently? Yes. But don't let labels mislead you. There are many ways to communicate. Winking is communicating. So is smiling, scowling, blushing. So is crying. So is love-making (of whatever degree).

In an eighth-grade English class, some of the students were falling backwards to be caught by trustworthy classmates. What does falling have to do with mastering their native language?

Some sensitivity training sessions may be conducted with children seated in a tight circle, sometimes on the floor, with no "barrier" (such as a table) separating them.

Self-awareness includes awareness of one's emotions, values and beliefs as well as physical awareness — awareness of one's own body. It doesn't take a great imagination to see the possible personality damage and social problems that could result from deliberate self-awareness "education."

To be aware of something means to be conscious of it. Self-awareness means self-consciousness. Who is more miserable than the self-conscious teen-ager? Self-awareness (or self-consciousness) may turn the teen-ager into an egomaniac (the braggart, the stuffed shirt, the conversation monopolizer) as one extreme — or into a miserable, self-conscious, introverted wallflower variety at the other end of the spectrum.

What can deliberate self-awareness education contribute to a child's mental health? Isn't the absence of self-consciousness more of an indication of mental health than self-consciousness? Teen-agers need to look out, not in. And most of all they need to look up.

In some school districts children in the lower elementary grades are being subjected to body and emotional awareness "education."

The possibility of psychological damage to sensitive children from group criticism is great. Furthermore, what difference does it make what the group thinks? We do not answer ultimately to the group. We answer to God.

Is homogenization of values and beliefs the goal? How can "group consensus" be reconciled with Christianity? Christians are admonished in the New Testament to: "Be not conformed to this world. . . ."

The process of changing attitudes and beliefs (and consequently behavior) involves three steps:

(1) *Unfreezing:* uprooting or dissolving values and standards which do not conform to the "desired" goal.

(2) *Changing:* helping the child develop new attitudes, beliefs or values which do conform to the predetermined goal.

(3) *Refreezing:* reinforcing the new attitudes, beliefs, and values.

The terms "unfreezing," "changing," and "refreezing" are used in the National Training Laboratories (NEA) manual, Selected Readings Series Five, *Issues in Human Relations Training* (1962).

"Emotionalism is the mode of operation in almost all sensitivity training groups. Intellectualizing is strictly forbidden. The rational components of values are ignored,"[29] another writer in *Educational Leadership* stated.

The green, fertile pastures of public education where young "social animals" are being trained, present seemingly irresistible and unsurpassed opportunities to those who fancy themselves qualified to serve as "shapers" of others. Here, the "animals" are not only captive, they are young and "flexible." There is less to be "unlearned" and "relearned," than would be the case with "rigid" adults. And, if enough of these young ones can be "shaped" and headed in the same predetermined direction, virtually the whole herd may be guided sheeplike down the primrose path where the change agent leadeth.

The "Behavior Shapers"

Operant conditioning is another form of behavioral control. The child can be expected to perform a particular task today if he received a reward when he completed the task yesterday and the day before, and the day before that. The reward is called *positive reinforcement*. The reward may be tangible — a lollipop or "tokens" that can be traded for some item the child wants. Or, the positive reinforcement may be an intangible, such as a compliment.

One psychologist has said that positive reinforcement — giving rewards for acceptable or desirable behavior — not only works with animals; it works "even better with humans." [30]

The common response tends to be: What's wrong with positive reinforcement? If it works, why not reward the child? After all, Sunday schools have given small awards to children for years for memorizing Scripture verses. And parents give rewards to children for doing small chores.

Numerous questions arise when positive reinforcement is used in public schools. What kind of learning is being reinforced? Suppose the assignments the child completes, in order to claim his reward, inculcate attitudes and beliefs that are in conflict with those he is being taught at home and church, thereby pulling the child in two directions at once, creating conflict? Confusion and indecision are the fruits of inward conflict. Is this conducive to "mental health"? Are the public schools contributing to psychological maladjustment in children? Are they driving a wedge between parents and their children? By whose design shall the children's behavior be molded? Who shall decide which attitudes and beliefs are to be inculcated?

Could answers to any of those questions be found in the following words written more than twenty years ago by behavioral psychologist B. F. Skinner [31] and uttered by one of the main characters in his fictitious *Walden Two?*

> When a science of behavior has once been achieved, there's no alternative to a planned society. We can't leave mankind to an accidental or biased control. [32]

> When you have once grasped the principle of positive reinforcement, you can enjoy a sense of unlimited power. It's enough to satisfy the thirstiest tyrant. [33]

According to a *Psychology Today* writer, in 1972, "Applied behavior analysis is a direct descendant of Skinnerian operant-conditioning experimentation." [34] Skinner is quoted in the same issue as stating, "The experimental analysis of behavior is an extremely advanced, rigorous science." [35]

Forty-one "Shapers at Work" (besides Skinner) are listed who "take Skinnerian principles out of the pigeon cage and put them into practice . . . . to change behavior in classrooms, kitchens, mental hospitals . . . and in the house next door." [36]

"Target subjects" of the shapers (beginning 1970) were listed as "whole schools, neighborhoods, whole counties, general public." And by year 2001, their "target subjects" include "everyone." [37]

In answer to the question "How do we choose the controllers?" [38] Skinner replied, "The controllers choose themselves. . . . Teachers, for example." [39] And Skinner admits, "There's nothing in behavior modification that guarantees that it will be used by good people." [40]

It is possible "for teachers to learn the essentials of applied behavior analysis in a week long workshop. . . ." [41]

Foregoing statements in this chapter should not be taken to mean that no psychiatrists or psychologists are Christians, or that all of them are anti-Christian. Some have taken a stand against sensitivity training, promotion of humanism and use of operant conditioning techniques in public schools.

Mrs. Mary Royer, M. S. (Res.) Psychology, was quoted in an Oregon newspaper in 1970 as warning parents, "In view of the fact that this type of human control [operant conditioning] can and will open the door to the unscrupulous, it is well for you to look closely at the new learning tools being introduced into the schools. . . ." [42] According to that newspaper article:

> Mrs. Royer stated that because it is relatively simple to administer, less easily defined, less easily identified . . . "operant conditioning is a completely insidious procedure and therefore has a substantially greater potential for the destruction of an individual than the mind-altering drugs. [43]
>
> "The concept that man is not free is essential to the application of the scientific technique of operant conditioning," she said, maintaining that when any person submits to, or is involuntarily submitted to the technique of operant conditioning, that individual is deprived of his freedom to the point that he becomes a puppet, or robot. [44]

The use of deliberate operant conditioning upon children in the captive audience of a classroom, without the knowledge and consent of parents, is completely untenable in a free society.

Behavior Modification for Hyperactive Children

Some of the old myths about why children aren't learning to read have been pretty well exposed. So new "reasons" must be found to "explain" the high percentage of non-readers and poor readers, which seems to persist in spite of spiraling school budgets and numerous innovations.

In recent years we have experienced a strange, new phenomenon. Like a horde of grasshoppers out of a clear blue sky, a sudden wave of hyperactive children has descended on the poor, overworked, bewildered teachers. Various and sundry possibilities ranging from vitamins to parents-with-psychiatric-problems have been offered as the explanation for this perplexing malady.

So, "problem behavior" creates or results in "learning disabilities."
What are some of the symptoms of hyperactivity or hyperkinesis? Hyperkinetics (most often boys) can't sit still, suffer from a short attention span, or like to walk around and disrupt others.

Proponents of a "Proposal for the Establishment of a Special Environment for Hyperactive Children" in one school district admitted, "It is extremely hard to pinpoint the types of behavior that could be placed and helped in a special environment."

The proposal also made it clear the class would not be "for mentally deficient children, but children of normal or above normal intelligence who have a behavior problem. . . ."

Some of the methods suggested that might help modify the child's behavior included: limiting auditory stimulation, "building simple plywood barriers for each child," and using social and token-type reinforcements. Each child would be given points for doing his work; he could have his lunch, recess, drinks, etc., only after adequate points were accumulated and turned in.

Self-evaluation by video tape was also suggested. ("Closed loop, video tape replay" was referred to as "a single example of dangerous, nonchemical behavior modification . . . a confrontation form of sensitivity training,"[45] in printed testimony in 1970 in a congressional hearing on behavior modification drugs and grammar school children.)

The proposal stated, "This program if implemented will need the help of a child psychologist or medical doctor. Many of the [hyperactive] children will at first be taking drugs, or will need some type of drug treatment."

About ten per cent of the children in grades one to five in that school had been designated as children who might "benefit" by such a program. Remember, these were children "of normal or above normal intelligence," and "many" of them would "need" drug treatment.

The amphetamines, commonly referred to as "speed," are among drugs administered to children for hyperactivity. How can this be correlated with "drug education" for elementary school children? How do you warn a child who is taking "speed" every day *not* to take speed?

Suppose the child's squirming or short attention span is caused by shoes that hurt his feet, an uncomfortable chair, or a physical ailment. Are drugs the ethical way to quiet him?

Suppose he is a healthy, strong boy whose bright mind and buoyant energy cannot be contained in a dull, boring "learning situation"? Should he be drugged into submission?

Does common sense cage a child with excessive energy in a plywood barrier and physically compel him into submission?

Some of these children might profit as much from an occasional sound paddling as from popping prescribed pills.

Many efficient teachers have, of course, used common sense approaches to discipline for years.

One of this nation's most brilliant men, Thomas Alva Edison, had a "behavior problem" when he started to school. His teacher called him "addled." [46] His mother, angered, took him out of school. [47] Fortunately for us, there were no compulsory education laws in Michigan (where he lived) in 1853. With today's system, he probably would have been "diagnosed" as "hyperactive." And we might have been burning kerosene lamps to this day.

The "Forecast for the 70's" published in 1969 in *Today's Education — NEA Journal*, stated:

> The basic role of the teacher will change noticeably. Ten years hence it should be more accurate to term him a "learning clinician." This title is intended to convey the idea that schools are becoming "clinics" whose purpose is to provide individualized psychosocial "treatment" for the student. . . . [48]

The article also forecast that in ten years "faculties will include. . . . biochemical therapist/pharmacists." [49]

Will it be "psychosocial" clinics instead of schools? "Clinicians" instead of teachers? "Therapy" or "treatment" instead of education? Will your children be their guinea pigs? Or are they already?

Planned Chaos?

Is it altogether coincidental that at the same time we have a rash of "hyperactive" children with "learning disabilities" (who need temporary reduction in sensory stimulation), that sensitivity training (including sensory awareness), is being promoted? That we hear a din of praise by educational innovators for "flexible scheduling," "open classrooms," "open plan schools," and "team teaching"?

And, no matter how worthless or potentially damaging an innovation may be, it will usually have its defenders. A newspaper article discussing "merits" of "the open school" concept mentions that, "According to a study . . . in Texas, eye difficulties and spinal curvature could be directly traced to the traditional desk and seating arrangement." [50]

If that was true, where does it leave youngsters in "open classrooms" who sit cross-legged on the floor with backs hunched, and little necks crimped or craned, as they strain to see charts higher than their eye level?

If we want to use the symbolism that "outmoded" fastened-down desks contributed to "rigid" thinking, and that movable desks symbolize or contribute to "flexible" thinking, let's use a little more symbolism. Perhaps the straight rows of desks were symbolic of, and contributed to, straight thinking. Perhaps the neat, orderly atmosphere represented and contributed to orderly thinking.

Years ago I read that you can tell what a person's mind is like by looking inside his dresser drawers. Is the confusion and clutter of some open plan schools a picture of the teachers' and children's minds?

The more persons there are in a room engaging in different activities at the same time, the more confusion and distractions there are likely to be. Concentration becomes increasingly difficult.

Is this "humane" environment a factor in the increase of "hyperactive" children with "learning disabilities"?

And what does confusion contribute to mental health?

Education That Heals

Educator Paul Brandwein, writing in the May, 1968, issue of *The Instructor*, said, "Education must heal. If it does not heal and make strong, it is not education."[51] In another publication he stated:

> The teacher is, in the last analysis, in the ministry of mercy.
> The teacher heals; if the classroom does not heal, it has no
> teacher, only an instructor. . . . Children do not always choose
> their parents well, or their heredity, or their environment, or
> their proper moment in history. Thus, above all, a teacher
> heals.[52]

Have you authorized your child's teacher to heal him? Of what? Does
the teacher have a license to practice anything other than teaching?

NOTES

1 'Behavioral Disorders May be Inheritable," (UPI), *Roseburg* (Ore.)
News-Review, April 25, 1972, (hereafter cited as Rosenthal, "Behavioral
Disorders").

2 *Ibid.*

3 *Brain-Washing: A Synthesis of the Russian Textbook on Psychopolitics,*
n.d., n.p. (distributed by Kenneth Goff, P.O. Box 116, Englewood, Colorado),
p. 33.

4 *Ibid.,* p. 58.

5 *Ibid.,* p. 33.

6 *Ibid.,* p. 6; the publication stated (and this was prior to 1936) that "the
tenets of Karl Marx, Pavlov, Lamarck, and the data of Dialectic Materialism"
had been placed in psychology textbooks in the United States. It further stated
that "As every chair of psychology in the United States is occupied by persons in
our connection, or who can be influenced by persons in our connection, the
consistent employment of such texts is guaranteed." (*Ibid.,* p. 53) Operatives
were advised: "Should anyone attempt to expose psychotherapy as a psychopolitical activity, the best defense is calling into question the sanity of the
attacker. The next best defense is authority. The next best defense is a validation
of psychiatric practices in terms of long and impressive figures." (On the same
page operatives were advised, "Not one of these cases cites need be real. . . .")
"The next best defense is the actual removal of the attacker by giving him, or
them, treatment sufficient to bring about a period of insanity for the duration of
the trial." (*Ibid.,* pp. 50, 51.) "It should become well-known that 'only the
insane attack psychiatrists.' . . .Should any whisper, or pamphlet, against
psychopolitical activities be published, it should be laughed into scorn, branded
an immediate hoax, and its perpetrator or publisher should be, at the first
opportunity branded as insane, and by the use of drugs the insanity should be

confirmed." (*Ibid.*, p. 52.)

7 Rousas J. Rushdoony, *The Myth of Over-population,* University Series: Historial Studies (Nutley, New Jersey: Craig Press, 1969), p. 45.

8 Rosenthal, "Behavioral Disorders."

9 *Ibid.*

10 D.L. Rosenhan, "On Being Sane in Insane Places," *Science,* Vol. 179, No 4070, January 19, 1973, p. 257.

11 *Ibid.*, p. 251.

12 *Ibid.*, p. 252.

13 *Ibid.*, p. 253.

14 *Ibid.*, p. 257.

15 *Ibid.*

16 Kenneth Goff, "The Battle for Your Mind," (mimeographed newsletter, Englewood, Colorado, n.d.), p. 2.

17 Albert Ellis,"The Case Against Religion," pamphlet (New York: Institute for Rational Living, Inc.; reprinted from Mensa Journal, No. 138, September, 1970).

18 *Ibid.*

19 G.B. Chisholm, "The Reestablishment of Peacetime Society: The Responsibility of Psychiatry," an address, second series William Alanson White Memorial Lectures, *The Psychiatry of Enduring Peace and Social Progress* (offprinted from *Psychiatry: Journal of the Biology and the Pathology of Interpersonal Relations,* ©1947 by The William Alanson White Psychiatric Foundation, Inc., Vol. 9, No. 1, February, 1946).

20 N.I.M.H. Computer print-out S-4564, Moore, Suicide-Professionals; 537-L3; Walter Freeman, *The Psychiatrist: Personalities and Patterns* (New York: Grune and Stratton, 1968), pp. 274-284.

21 N.I.M.H. Computer print-out S-4564, Moore, Suicide-Professionals; 20150-L3; *Medical World News* 8(23); 28-29, 1967.

22 II Tim. 1:7.

23 Bill Popejoy, "I Read It In a Book," *The Pentecostal Evangel,* No. 3057, December 10, 1972, p. 7.

24 Jim Wood, "Educators Who Feel Their Way to Self Knowledge," *San Francisco* (California) *Examiner,* July 19, 1969, p. 13.

25 *Ibid.*

26 John Guernsey, "Educators Learn Sensitivity, Kill Inhibitions," The (Portland) *Oregonian,* December 30, 1968.

27 Harold C. Wells, " 'To Get Beyond the Words. . .' ", *Educational Leadership,* Vol. 28, No. 3, December 1970, p. 241.

28 *Ibid.*, p. 242.

29 Clifford H. Edwards, "Sensitivity Training and Education: A Critique," *Educational Leadership*, Vol. 28, No. 3, December, 1970, p. 261.

30 James Dobson, *Dare to Discipline*, paperback (co-published by Tyndale House, Publishers, Wheaton, Illinois, and Regal Books, G/L Publications, Glendale, California; ©1970 by Tyndale House, Publishers), P. 54.

31 B.F. Skinner, author of the controversial book *Beyond Freedom and Dignity*, was presented the Humanist of the Year Award for 1972 by the American Humanist Association. His name is listed in *The Humanist* magazine (1972) as a member of the editorial board of that magazine.

32 B.F. Skinner, *Walden Two*, 1969 printing with new preface by author (The Macmillan Company; Collier-Macmillan Limited, London; Collier-Macmillan Canada, Ltd., Toronto, Ontario, 1969; © B.F. Skinner, 1948), P. 264.

33 *Ibid.*

34 Kenneth Goodall, "Shapers at Work," *Psychology Today*, Vol. 6, No. 6, November, 1972, p. 58 (hereafter cited as Goodall, 'Shapers at Work").

35 Elizabeth Hall, "Will Success Spoil B.F. Skinner?", *Psychology Today*, Vol. 6, No. 6, November, 1972, p. 66 (hereafter cited as Hall, "Will Success Spoil B.F. Skinner?").

36 Goodall, "Shapers at Work"; quotation from p. 53; shapers listed pp. 58 to 63.

37 *Ibid.*, p. 62.

38 Hall, "Will Success Spoil B.F. Skinner?", p. 72

39 *Ibid.*

40 *Ibid.*, p. 130.

41 Goodall, "Shapers at Work," p. 134.

42 "Operant Conditioning Called Dangerous Tool,' *Hillsboro* (Ore.) *Argus*, October 1, 1970.

43 *Ibid.*

44 *Ibid.*

45 Statement by Marilyn P. Desaulniers for the Special Studies Subcommittee, House Committee on Government Operations, House of Representatives, Ninety-First Congress, Second Session, September 29, 1970, *Federal Involvement in the Use of Behavior Modification Drugs on Grammar School Children of the Right to Privacy Inquiry*, p. 146.

46 Winifred Wise Graham, *Thomas Alva Edison*, Real People series (Evanston, Illinois and Elmsford, New York: Harper and Row, Publishers, 1950), p. 2.

47 *Ibid.*

48 Harold G. Shane and June Grant Shane, "Forecast for the 70's," *Today's Education — NEA Journal*, January, 1969, p. 31.

49 *Ibid.*, p. 32.

50 Helen Hennessy, NEA Women's Editor, Opening Up Education, The Classroom As A Learning Tool," *Roseburg* (Ore.) *News-Review,* May 8, 1973.

51 Paul Brandwein, "School System of the Future. .", *The Instructor,* Vol LXXVII, No. 9, May, 1968, p. 43.

52 Paul F. Brandwein, *Notes on Teaching the Social Sciences: Concepts and Values* (Harcourt Brace Jovanovich, Inc., ©1969); (portions of the essay reprinted from *Toward a Discipline of Responsible Consent: Elements in a Strategy for Teaching Social Sciences in the Elementary School* by Paul F. Brandwein, ©1969 by Harcourt Brace Jovanovich, Inc.), p. 10.

6

TEACHING CHILDREN "TO COPE" WITH LIFE

No one can say that shackles and obstacles are fatal barriers to success. They have proven to be *incentives*. Perfect equipment does not always win the battle . . . .Here is a man with every favorable circumstance — intelligence, social background, wealth — whose life miserably fails. Here is another, fettered at every step, physically misshaped, without means, with very little schooling — fighting his way with an unconquerable spirit toward glorious success.

. . . C. M. Ward

"Schools can do a lot of things, but they must prepare students to survive," said Dr. Dale Parnell, Oregon Superintendent of Public Instruction, in 1971. He believed students should pass "real life" tests as a requirement for high school graduation. Some of the categories included in his "survival" education were communication skills, arithmetic, and career education. He believed graduates should also know how to read a barometer and a geographic map, how to determine gasoline mileage per gallon, how to swim, and how to repair a broken light cord. And a girl should know how to change an automobile tire. [1]

"My whole thesis here," he was quoted as saying, "is that we've got to help students develop confidence in themselves that they can cope, that they have the ability, the skills, the understanding to cope with life. [2]

"Real life" skills don't have to be taught at school, he conceded. "If they can learn it off television and sit home, fine." [3]

Are these ideas valid?

I have driven thousands of miles in the last twenty years and I've never changed a tire (nor even put air into one). I've never read a barometer nor repaired a broken light cord.

This is not to say that for a girl to know how to change a tire isn't helpful or worthwhile, or that the ability to repair a broken light cord isn't commendable. But is mastery of skills like these really the criteria for "coping" with life?

Thousands of grime-laden, drug-stupored hippies learned to change an automobile tire, swim, and read a road map. (Some of them can even read and write.) Yet many of them have not "survived" socially, morally, mentally, or physically. Did "real life" learning provide the answers they so desperately needed?

Granted, it is important to know how to perform menial and trivial tasks. But, is this the business of tax-supported public education?

Granted, it is necessary and important that young people know how to earn a living. One of the most likely contributions public schools could make toward that goal is to make certain every normal child learns to read and write fluently and masters computational skills.

Many would probably agree with Dr. Parnell that students, as a prerequisite for high school graduation, should be tested in communications skills (if by that he means reading and writing and not sensitivity training) and in arithmetic. On second thought, why should all normal children not have mastered these skills as a requirement for promotion from the eighth grade — rather than from the twelfth grade?

How does a person learn "to cope" with life? Does man — man who was created in the image of God — learn "to cope" with life by learning to change a tire or name a balanced diet? Is knowing how to earn a very affluent living any guarantee the person knows how "to cope" with life? Would ulcer frequency and alcoholism among the wealthy indicate otherwise?

Are training and education the same? Typists, mechanics, and plumbers (as examples) may be thoroughly trained and highly proficient in their skills, and yet remain abysmally uneducated in the broad liberal sense. Their own narrow specialities may be virtually all they know. That is vocational training.

Rev. Edmund Opitz, a staff member of the Foundation for Economic Education, has said:

> It is needful that men possess such skills as the ability to lay bricks [and] cut hair. . . . But while the possession of such skills is desirable and important, their exercise is not the distinctive mark of an educated man. It is true, however, that an educated man ought to have a quiverful of such and similar

talents. . . . But this is merely to say that a man ought to be trained as well as educated. [4]

Might we also add that a person ought to be educated as well as trained? In twelve long years in the public schools, isn't there time for considerable amounts of both?

Suppose a person is both educated in the broad secular sense and also trained in various important skills. Are these alone sufficient to enable him "to cope" with life? Most certainly not.

Sickness, sudden financial loss, death of loved ones, unemployment, loneliness, disappointments in love affairs — these are some of the severe storms of life that can strike any of us without warning.

Then there are the day-to-day frictions and annoyances — an unhappy marriage, the neighbor's dogs, prolonged poverty. These are the drippy faucets of life that grate one's nerves and wear one's patience threadbare.

Some are both uneducated and unskilled and yet are geniuses at "coping" both with life's sudden, severe storms and with prolonged irritations. Others are both well-educated and highly skilled in respectable professions and yet are overwhelmed when confronted with severe pressures or personal loss.

The ability "to cope" is the ability to maintain emotional stability and moral integrity in the face of sudden, severe adversity or under prolonged irritation. Secular education and job-training alone can never equip a person with the spiritual stamina necessary "to cope" with the great problems of life.

"Coping" is not only remaining emotionally and morally intact in the face of the worst that life may bring, it is also handling the best material blessings life may bring — wealth, friends, travel, health, love, fame — without succumbing to arrogance, selfishness, or moral decadence.

Why do some "cope" with life's sudden, violent storms while others crack and crumble? Why are some able to maintain their integrity and humility when life brings fame and fortune while others use their prosperity unwisely?

The Apostle Paul knew the secret. He said, "I have learned, in whatsoever state I am, therewith to be content." [5] He knew how "both to be full and to be hungry, both to abound and to suffer need." [6] That is coping. His wellsprings never ran dry. He had tapped the Source.

Having an abundance of material possessions, or having the skills and knowledge to acquire them, is not the key to coping with life: ". . .for a man's life consisteth not in the abundance of the things which he possesseth." [7]

"Freedom from guilt, assurance of purpose, the experience of God's love — only these realities can meet the needs of today's restless, frustrated, despairing youth. [8] . . . Who are you?. . . How can you achieve true happiness?. . . Where will you go after you die?. . Only the Word of God can give you the answer." [9]

The former Oregon State Superintendent of Public Instruction, and those who parrot the "real life learning" line as a prescription for coping with life are, no doubt, sincere and well-intentioned. But their prescription is inadequate.

Students can be taught welding and woodworking — or how to change an automobile tire — without reference to God. But this kind of "education," even as a utilitarian tool, may prove short-sighted. Our rapidly changing technology may render "survival" skills such as these obsolete tomorrow. At any rate, let's not pretend that mastering menial skills — as important as they may seem at the moment — will prepare anyone to cope with life.

In the words of Professor Emeritus of English Literature, E. Merrill Root, "It is not enough to have welfare and security; it is not enough to eat and sleep and reproduce." [10] This is true because man is not made in the image of an animal. He has another dimension.

Teen-agers, in order to be able to cope with the storms and stresses of life in the 'seventies — like teen-agers of any other decade — need an Anchor, a North Star. Some will counter that the schools cannot teach children there is an Anchor. My reply is educators should not say, then, they are teaching children to cope with life. How can an educational system that, for the most part ignores the Source of all life, (implying He is unimportant — if He does indeed exist) — possibly teach children to cope with life?

NOTES

1 "Dr. Dale Parnell: 'Real Life' Learning Needed by Graduates," *Roseburg* (Ore.) *News-Review,* September 8, 1971.

2 *Ibid.*

3 *Ibid.*

4 Rev. Edmund A. Opitz, from Introduction to *Intellectual Schizophrenia Culture, Crisis and Education,* by Rousas J. Rushdoony; International Library, Philosophical and Historical Studies (Philadelphia, Pennsylvania: Presbyterian and Reformed Publishing Company, 1971; ©1961), pp. xx, xxi.

5 Phil. 4:11b.

6 Phil. 4:12b.

7 Luke 12:15b.

8 Richard W. DeHaan, *The Generation Gap,* pamphlet (Grand Rapids, Michigan: Radio Bible Class, ©1969), p. 15.

9 *Ibid.*

10 E. Merrill Root; "The Type of Education Which Produced Great American Leadership," an address (*News and Views,* Vol. 26, No. 3, Wheaton, Illinois, March, 1963), p. 2.

HOW SCIENTIFIC IS THE THEORY OF EVOLUTION?

The probability of life originating from accident is comparable to the probability of an unabridged dictionary resulting from an explosion in a printing shop.

. . . Biologist Edwin Conklin

There are two predominate explanations (with variations of each) as to how the earth was formed and how life began. One is the Genesis account of direct acts of creation in a particular period of time by a Divine and Omnipotent Creator; the other is the theory of evolution.

For decades multitudes of children in public schools have been permitted — usually required — to consider only one of the two predominate views. For that reason a critical book on public education would be incomplete without a discussion of both predominate explanations of the origin of the earth and of man.

What does the word "evolution" mean to most people?

A proponent of the General Theory of Evolution, which is the amoeba to man thesis, would state that all living things in the world have arisen from a single source that came from an inorganic beginning. Thus, according to the General Theory of Evolution, the first living cell "evolved" into complex multi-cellular forms of life; these gave rise to all forms of inverte-brates; in turn, invertebrates "evolved" into vertebrates; fish into amphibia, amphibia into reptiles, reptiles into birds and mammals, early mammals into primates, and finally primates "evolved" into man. Unmistakably this is the basic meaning of the term "evolution" for most people. [1]

Few people in our educated society would believe a skyscraper could "evolve" without the design of an architect, regardless of how favorable the circumstances or the length of time allowed.

Yet, the prevailing philosophy among many educators, scientists, and other intellectuals is that all the intricate marvels of nature working in beautiful order and harmony, "evolved" without the purpose or design of a Creator. "That such deception can be so universal is a sobering testimony to the abysmal darkness in which modern man lives." [2]

The blame for the prevalence of this myth among the general populace in our day can be laid primarily on the doorstep of the public school house.

The late Richard M. Weaver said, ". . .no education is innocent of an attitude toward the existing world. In the way that it explains the inter-relationships of phenomena and our relationships toward them, education will reveal beliefs about creation." [3] For modern gnostic educators "the universe is not a work of divine omnipotence." [4] As Weaver points out, their utterances reveal what their suppositions are. [5]

Many public school teachers would not go so far as to make outright verbal attacks in the classroom on the Genesis account of creation or to deny the existence of a Supernatural God. However, when the theory of evolution is taught exclusively, and the Genesis account is completely ignored, this constitutes a subtle attack on the Scriptural account of creation and therefore on Christianity itself.

"Bias may be manifested, and produced, not only by what one says and does, but also by what one does not say and do." [6]

A very effective way to indoctrinate (particularly young children) is to present to them only one viewpoint, and simply fail to mention that another possibility exists.

To teach the theory of evolution exclusively, as even a possibility, calls into question the Divine inspiration and accuracy of the Genesis account. For if the earth evolved and man arrived via the animal chain, then Genesis is not true. This, in turn, raises questions as to the authenticity and accuracy of the entire Bible. If one portion is unreliable, how can any portion be accepted as Truth? To undercut or destroy a child's belief in the Genesis account is to weaken the cornerstone of his faith in any of the Scriptures. In the words of Rushdoony:

> Anyone who denies the authority of Scripture at one point has denied it at all points. If we assert that we can set aside the six-day creation doctrine, we have asserted our supremacy over Scripture. *Our mind* and *our* convenience now have a higher

authority than the Bible, so that we have denied its authority totally and asserted our authority instead. If we claim the right at any point to set aside Scripture, we have established ourselves as the higher authority at *every* point. Clearly, therefore, the question of authority is at stake in *Genesis* 1: God or man? Whose word is authoritative and final? [7]

Theistic Evolution

Some say they believe God created the earth and man through the processes of evolution. This is known as theistic evolution.

Genesis is very clear that at a specific time-point in history "God created all things in the way He wanted them, each with its own structure and functions according to His own sovereign purpose for it. . . . Genesis One, for example, indicates that at least ten major categories of organic life were specially created. . . ." [8]

These categories [9] are:

Plant Kingdom	Animal Kingdom	Mankind
grass	sea monsters	man
herbs	other marine animals	
fruit trees	birds	
	beasts	
	cattle	
	crawling animals	

Evolutionists claim the earth and life came into being through an extended process, taking possibly billions of years, and that the process of change is still occurring. Genesis teaches: "Thus the heavens and the earth were finished, and all the host of them. And on the seventh day God ended His work." [10]

To believe the theory of evolution means you can believe living things came into being from dead substance without outside help and that one kind came from another kind.

The theory of evolution teaches progression from lower to higher and more complicated types. This is not only in contradiction with Scripture, it is also in contradiction with the Second Law of Thermodynamics, which maintains there is a trend in all physical things toward running down and wearing out.

Some will argue that the process of creation could have taken billions of years because perhaps the length of days was different then than now.

There is no scientific certainty as to how long it took.

"If God actually employed such a coding technique in writing Genesis One" [11] whereby the word *day* might mean millions of years, why would He "withhold the key to the code from all His holy prophets and apostles" [12] and leave it to atheistic or agnostic scientists to interpret the "facts" to Christians in our generation?

Evolutionists believe man shares a common ancestor with primates such as the gorilla. This belief is not compatible with the Genesis account of separate creations of individual kinds, in the beginning.

The Biblical account tells us the first man, Adam, was created as a direct act of God on a particular day in time. Because Adam was the handiwork of God, created in God's own image, we can believe he was perfect in form — physically and genetically perfect — one of the most handsome men imaginable. We can assume his wife, likewise formed by a deliberate act of God, was gracious and beautiful. Since they were created as adults, in God's own image, we know they were intelligent and immediately capable of intelligent, verbal communication.

To believe the evolutionary theory means we can believe the first men to inhabit the earth were crude-looking, ape-like creatures of low mentality who might be visualized as sitting on their haunches with blank looks on their faces, making strange babbling sounds. This description of the first men is a flagrant insult to the Creator who made the first man in His own image.

Clearly, Genesis and the theory of evolution are not compatible. "Evolution is a theory which is radically hostile to biblical religion." [13]

The Basis for a New Morality

The implications of the theory of evolution are far-reaching. If man evolved from a speck of sea slime, he was not created in the image of God as stated in Genesis.

If man is only a graduate beast, as evolutionists claim — if God did not create man — then God (if there is a God) has no claim on man. If God is not man's Creator, what is man's responsibility to God? Why should man obey God's laws — if indeed there is a God?

With denial of authority of the Holy Bible, the foundation of moral absolutes crumbles.

If man evolved and is just another animal — a social animal — his only responsibility is to himself and to his fellow "animals." Morality (the concept of right and wrong) is whatever the individual or the group concedes it to be. Man is not "fallen" or sinful as Genesis teaches. An evolved animal has no need of a Savior. "Take away the first three chapters of Genesis, and you cannot maintain a true Christian position nor give Christianity's answers."[14]

With moral absolutes (God's Laws) relegated as outdated religious "folklore," the door is left wide open for the whole foggy, relativist dogma: no certainty, only probability; no black or white, only shifting shades of gray.

"The convincing thing about evolution is not that it proves man's origins or even gives anything resembling a possible theory but that it dispenses with God"[15] as Creator.

If man was created in God's own image, as Genesis states, then man is indeed responsible to his Maker, and there are Divine Guidelines for man's behavior.

Scientific Aspects

Those not interested in the religious objections to the theory of evolution might be interested in the credibility of the theory itself in the light of recent scientific data.

In December, 1971, Dr. John N. Moore, a scientist from Michigan State University, presented a paper to the Society for the Study of Evolution at the annual meeting of the American Association for the Advancement of Science (A.A.A.S.) in Philadelphia.

The purpose of his paper was "to accomplish a careful . . . examination as to how close a 'fit' may be drawn between the commonly accepted theoretical monophylogenetic [evolutionary] explanation of relationships of animals and of plants and known empirical data at this point in time at the end of 1971, after over 70 years of genetic and cytological research."[16]

His examination included:[17]

    (1) Protein Phylogenies Test

    (2) Structural and Numerical Mutations Test

    (3) Gene Mutations Test

    (4) Chromosome Number and Quality Test

    (5) Fossil Record Test

In the section "Chromosome Number and Quality Test," Dr. Moore stated:

Upon close examination of these data on chromosome counts in animals and in plants, it would seem quite appropriate to conclude that the currently popular imagined transformational pattern of phylal relationships, called the monophyletic [one common ancestry] scheme, is *more illogical than biological.*

Other important points made in his paper include these:

No new traits come from gene mutations.[19]

Significant breeding gaps exist between *all* major groups of animals, and between *all* major groups of plants.[20]

Absolutely no *genetic* connections are ever established between major groups of living things by means of any mechanisms involving ploidy and chromosomal rearrangements.[21]

That inviolate *genetic* barriers exist between major groups of living things may be stated conclusively on the basis of available *genetic* evidences. Unbridgeable breeding gaps are known.[22]

Upon rigorous examination and analysis, any dogmatic assertion, as an empirical *fact,* that gene mutations are the raw material for any evolutionary process involving natural selection is an utterance of a *myth.*[23]

Dr. Moore notes we could logically assume an increase would occur in chromosome number as a characteristic of increased complexity on the basis of the monophyletic [evolutionary] explanation. His study indicates that chromosome counts (modified to show 2n values) are: 62 for a donkey; 46 for a man. Frogs have more DNA (in 10^{-12} gram) per haploid chromosome complement (7.5), than man (with 3.2).[24] He states:

Based upon a careful, five-fold examination, no empirically demonstrable data can be found which can "fit" the commonly, popularly accepted monophyletic explanation of relationship in diversity among animals or among plants.[25]

Textbook authors and professional biologists, who interpret empirical data through an "exclusive" monophyletic viewpoint, are doing so in a selected indoctrinaire attitude far removed from careful examination of real data.[26]

Dr. Moore does not recommend removing the teaching of the evolutionary theory from school curricula. "Evolution must be mentioned," he says, "since it is such an ancient idea of men. . . ."[27] First causes become "the primary concern of theologians, metaphysicians, and philosophers. [28] And based on a strict point of view regarding the basic assumption of cause and effect *no* discussion of 'origins' should be included in a science course. A search for 'origins' necessarily partakes of a search for first causes, which most scholars will agree is beyond the core aspect of scientific activity as defined by the problem-hypothesis-test process." [29]

It seems logical to ask, then, if the theory of evolution is to be taught at all in public schools, why shouldn't it be properly labelled and taught as "philosophy"? But, Dr. Moore explained, science teachers insist upon exploring "origins" and first causes. That being the case, it is his view that the creationist (Genesis) account of origins, as well as the evolutionist view, should be taught in public schools. [30]

> If such a two-way treatment of . . . interpretation of possible relationships of major groups of animals and major groups of plants is practiced by textbook authors, and if such is followed by teachers and professors, then selected indoctrination of another generation of bright, independently thinking students regarding phylogeny might be avoided. [31]

"But," you say, "we can't teach Genesis. That's religion."

What do you think the theory of evolution is?

An "incredible religion," [32] in the words of Dr. Moore.

Neither evolution nor Divine creation can be tested by the criteria of scientific method. The origin of the earth occurred in the distant past and cannot be observed nor is it experimentally repeatable. Experimental repeatability is vital to scientific method.

Both the Genesis account of creation and the theory of evolution are religions because faith is required to believe either. Evolution requires faith in man's ideas; Genesis requires faith in God's written Word.

> At the base of evolutionary faith is the adoption of eternal matter with the inherent quality of spontaneous generation of life. . . .

> Opposed to that, then, is the admitted faith commitment of an eternal God who supplied the plan for life and the energy for life. . . . [33]

Why do some evolutionists so vehemently oppose an objective study of the Genesis account of creation (in addition to the evolutionary theory) in the classroom? Are they afraid students may come to see it really takes more faith to believe in the humanistic theory of evolution than in the Genesis record?

The religion of humanism leans heavily on belief in the process of evolution. The second tenet of Humanist Manifesto I (1933) states, "Humanism believes that man is a part of nature and that he has emerged as the result of a continuous process." [34]

In any public school where the humanistic theory of evolution is taught and the Biblical Genesis account is ignored, the religion of Secular Humanism is clearly favored and promoted over Christianity. "If teachers center their teaching exclusively on evolutionary ideas about origins, they could be charged as guilty of establishing a *religion of humanism.*" [35]

NOTES

1 John N. Moore, *Should Evolution Be Taught?* (Pamphlet, fourth printing, July, 1972), p. 5 (hereafter cited as Moore, *Should Evolution Be Taught?*).

2 W.F. Elgin, "The Beginning of Wisdom," *Roseburg* (Ore.) *News-Review,* April 17, 1971.

3 Richard M. Weaver, *Visions of Order: The Cultural Crisis of Our Time,* paperback ed., (Baton Rouge: Louisiana State University Press, 1964; manufactured in U.S.A. by Vail-Ballou Press, Inc., Binghamton, N.Y.), p. 120.

4 *Ibid.,* p. 121.

5 *Ibid.*

6 Nicholas Wolterstorff, *Religion and the Schools,* A Reformed Journal Monograph, (Grand Rapids: William B. Eerdmans Publishing Co., 1965, 1966; first appeared in slightly different form in *Reformed Journal,* Grand Rapids), p. 22.

7 Rousas John Rushdoony, *The Mythology of Science,* paperback ed., University Series, Historical Studies (Nutley, N.J.: The Craig Press, ©1967; second printing, September, 1968), pp. 45, 46, (hereafter cited as Rushdoony: *Mythology*).

8 Henry M. Morris, "Theistic Evolution," *Creation Research Society Quarterly,* Vol. 8, No. 4, March, 1972, p. 270.

9 *Ibid.*

10 Genesis 2:1, 2a.

11 Henry M. Morris, *The Remarkable Birth of Planet Earth,* paperback ed.

(San Diego: Institute for Creation Research, 1972), p. 83.

12 *Ibid.*

13 Rushdoony, *Mythology*, p. 49.

14 Francis A. Schaeffer, *The God Who Is There*, paperback ed. (Third American printing, Downers Grove, Ill.: Inter-Varsity Press, December, 1969, with permission from Hodder and Stoughton Limited, England; ©1968 by Francis A. Schaeffer), p. 104.

15 Rushdoony, *Mythology*, p. 48.

16 John N. Moore, "On Chromosomes, Mutations, and Phylogeny," (mimeographed paper read before Society for the Study of Evolution Session, December 27, 1971, 138th Annual American Association for Advancement of Science Meetings, Philadelphia, Pa.), p. 2 (hereafter cited as Moore, "Phylogeny").

17 *Ibid.*, see pp. 2, 3, 4, 5, 8.

18 *Ibid.*, p. 7.

19 *Ibid.*, p. 9.

20 *Ibid.*, p. 3.

21 *Ibid.*, pp. 3, 4.

22 *Ibid.*, p. 4.

23 *Ibid.*, p. 5.

24 *Ibid.*, see pp. 6, 7.

25 *Ibid.*, p. 9.

26 *Ibid.*

27 Moore, *Should Evolution Be Taught?*, p. 2.

28 *Ibid.*, p. 4.

29 *Ibid.*, p. 25.

30 *Ibid.*, see p. 26.

31 Moore, "Phylogeny," p. 10.

32 "Darwin's Evolution Theory Under Fire," *Los Angeles Herald Examiner*, December 27, 1971.

33 Reg Crowder quoting John N. Moore, "Controversy of Evolution Still Debated," *Hollywood* (Fla.) *Sun-Tattler*, May 19, 1973.

34 "A Humanist Manifesto" (published in *The New Humanist*, Vol. VI, No. 3, in 1933; *The New Humanist* ceased publication in 1936); "Humanist Manifesto" reproduced in its entirety in *Guidelines for Moral Instruction in California Schools*, (a report accepted by the California State Board of Education May 9, 1969), see pp. 37-40 of Guidelines.

35 John N. Moore, "Teach Creation in School," *Child Evangelism*, Vol. XXXI, No. 8, September, 1972, p. 10.

8

PRESCRIPTIONS FOR SOCIAL PROBLEMS

If God is the Creator, then man, the family and society must serve Him and move in terms of His law, *but if society is the maker of man and his family, then man and the family must move in terms of true society and become agencies thereof. Man is bound by the laws of his nature and of his creation, and if man is a social product, then the law of his being is the law of the pack, and the greater the pack the truer its law.*

. . . Rousas J. Rushdoony
The Messianic Character of American Education

Sociology is the study of human behavior in society. It may be included in, or come under the label of, social studies, social science, or modern problems.

Problems children may study and to which they may practice applying problem-solving techniques include personal problems and social problems. Social problems are individual problems multiplied and compounded.

To understand man's behavioral and social problems, it is necessary to understand something about the origin (and consequently the nature) of man. As stated in a previous chapter, there are two predominate, irreconcilable views as to the origin of man: the theory of evolution and the belief that man is the product of a deliberate Divine act that occurred at a particular time-point in history.

Prescriptions to solve man's behavioral and social problems can hardly be the same for both beliefs when the basic presuppositions differ so widely.

Wrong prescriptions resulting from misdiagnosis may not only be worthless as a cure, they may be devastating by further complicating the problem.

Consider some of the current social problems in the United States. For every three marriages, there is more than one divorce. Among us are nine million alcoholics. Use of other dangerous drugs is rampant. Venereal disease has reached epidemic proportions. Hundreds of thousands of helpless unborn innocents are slaughtered without mercy each year, by men traditionally dedicated to saving life.

In addition, the following statistics [1] were issued in September, 1974, by the F.B.I. as estimated crime in the United States, for the year of 1973:

Murder	19,510
Forcible rape	51,000
Robbery	382,680
Aggravated assault	416,270
Burglary	2,540,900
Larceny-theft	4,304,400
Auto theft	923,600

What is the solution? Does psychology have the answer? Sociology? Secular education?

What is man's basic root problem from which such behavior stems?

If each of the persons involved in the tragedies and crimes mentioned above had been living consistently in compliance with God's Absolutes as recorded in His written Word, how many of these social and personal tragedies would have occurred? *Not a single one.*

If your answer is right, you can be reasonably certain your basic premise or presupposition is correct. What is the premise? That man is the deliberate handiwork of God, created in His own Image, and therefore has a moral responsibility to His Maker. When his relationship with his Maker is right, his relationships with his fellow men and himself will be right.

"Man does what he does because he is what he is." [2] Man's relations with his fellow men go awry when his relationship with God is awry. "The restoration of harmony between man and God is inseparable from the restoration of harmony between man and man." [3] The problem is not in man's environment. "The problem is in man, and the answer is in God." [4]

All vital questions of the human family are already answered in the Word of God. [5]

The Scriptures cannot be equalled in the study of sociology.

Man's inhumanity to man has always been a blight on our race simply because so few have been willing to read and follow the precepts of God's Word. It solves the ill of discrimination. It gives accurate instructions concerning women's lib. It charts the course for the ideal courtship and marriage. [6]

The general belief is: correct the social injustices, move the stone of ignorance, take away the causes of misunderstanding, and man will "straighten up and fly right." This would all be very wonderful if man himself *were* basically right. He, man, is the crux of the whole matter. [7]

Dr. Henry M. Morris, scientist, has declared:

Since man is made "in the image of God," his actions must be intrinsically connected with this fact and its implications. He has rebelled against the divine fellowship for which he was created, and the behaviour of unregenerate man is fundamentally dependent upon this fact, and not upon chemical and physical phenomena or upon those characteristics . . . which are shared with animals. A real science of human behaviour must necessarily be built upon the great Biblical truths of the Fall, redemption, and reconciliation, and certainly the Bible is our only textbook of these areas of science! [8]

Dr. Cornelius Van Til, philosopher and author, maintains, "Whatever is in accord with Scripture is educative; whatever is not in accord with it is miseducative." [9]

Are social and personal problem-solving as taught in most public schools today educative or miseducative? What kind of solutions to social problems does public education offer or suggest? Are children being led to believe that crime is due to poverty or other environmental factors? That socialist programs such as government housing are the answer?

It is on the presupposition that man is an evolved animal that virtually all modern educational philosophy, anthropology, sociology, and psychology proceed.

H. Edward Rowe, editor of *Applied Christianity* magazine, has stated Humanism *"might be defined as man's effort to solve his problems and shape his society apart from God.* [10] Humanism is man's effort to eliminate God from his thinking, and to live as if God did not exist. It is man attempting to solve his problems and to construct his own heaven on earth apart from Almighty God." [11]

By what criterion are children in public schools being taught to solve social and personal problems? By what method? When explanations and solutions to man's behavior and social problems are taught exclusively within a humanistic framework in tax-supported public schools, can the bias favoring the religion of Humanism over Christianity be denied?

NOTES

1 *Crime in the United States, 1973, Uniform Crime Reports,* issued by Clarence M. Kelley, Director, Federal Bureau of Investigation, U.S. Department of Justice, Washington, D.C. 20535, for release Friday AM, September 6, 1974, p. 1.

2 "Cleaning Up the Prodigal's Pig Pen . . . But Leaving the Prodigal As He Is," *Last Day Messenger* (quoting Dr. Henry Grube, in *The Midweek Message*), Vol. X, No. 5, September-October, 1972, p. 8, (hereafter cited as Grube: *Last Day Messenger*).

3 Nicholas Wolterstorff, *Religion and the Schools: A Reformed Journal Monograph* (Grand Rapids, Michigan: William B. Eerdmans Publishing Co., ©1965, 1966; first appeared in slightly different form in the *Reformed Journal*), p. 10.

4 Rousas John Rushdoony, *Chalcedon Report No. 88,* December, 1972, p. 4.

5 Bill Popejoy, "I Read It In a Book," *The Pentecostal Evangel,* No. 3057, December 10, 1972, p. 7.

6 *Ibid.*

7 Grube: *Last Day Messenger,* p. 8.

8 Henry M. Morris, *Studies in the Bible and Science* (Grand Rapids, Michigan: Baker Book House; ©1966 by Presbyterian and Reformed Publishing Company), p. 117 (quotation is from chapter entitled "The Bible *is* a Textbook of Science" which appeared as an article in two parts in October, 1964, and January, 1965, issues of *Bibliotheia Sacra.*).

9 Cornelius Van Til, *The Dilemma of Education* (Presbyterian and Reformed Publishing Company, June, 1956; first edition published by National Union of Christian Schools), p. 33.

10 H. Edward Rowe, *Humanism,* supplement to Christian Economics, n.d.

11 H. Edward Rowe, "What is Humanism?" *Applied Christianity,* Vol. 2, No. 8, August, 1973, p. 25.

9

LET'S ANALYZE READING PROGRAMS — NOT CHILDREN

Dull discipline of the three R's was disturbing to little Johnny's ego. So we got real scientific and went to work on the Poor Little Kid and his Id, with the result that today hardly any school that really is a school is without a class in remedial reading. It would save considerable money if the class were held in the very highest level of our teachers' colleges and were called "Remedial Thinking."

. . . Charles H. Brower

"A Giant Step Backward"

Nineteen years ago Dr. Rudolf Flesch, in *Why Johnny Can't Read,* stated educators "would hardly say out loud that they would postpone the teaching of reading until the age of ten or fifteen. They know very well that people wouldn't stand for it." [1]

It appears some educators have now "progressed" to the point they would dare say it out loud. Consider, for example, the following statements taken from a letter to the editor of a Coos Bay newspaper in 1971, written by an Oregon grade school principal:

I think we have reached the point where the secondary schools face the problem of their students just as the lower grades have done. Many of these students will never be fluent readers and they should be offered a vocational program to compensate for that. Many students at an older age will respond to reading once they have matured and see the need. What is wrong with teaching reading on the secondary level to those who have the ability, interest and maturity for it? [2]

That principal seems to be echoing the sentiments of certain professors around the country who have doubts about the importance of teaching children to read in the early grades.

Various issues of the Council for Basic Education *Bulletin* have cited

67

examples of such thinking:

Social studies, rather than reading, should be emphasized, one professor of education believes. (Reading isn't necessary for taking field trips, talking to "resource" people, and discussing "problem pictures.")

Reading in the early grades has been called a "sacred cow" by the dean of one University School of Education.

Two other influential professors seem to "fear that literacy may result in beliefs they [the professors] detest," according to a *Bulletin* writer.

Then, there is the psychologist who believes junior high level is soon enough to teach reading. (That would help lessen the likelihood of children tasting academic failure in their tender young years.)

Such thinking on the part of influential professors raises numerous questions. What are all those children doing 900 to 1,000 or more hours per year, between first grade and junior or senior high school? If they can't read, then history, geography, grammar, and science are all but impossible. Or does this explain the cry for more and more dollars for expensive audio-visual aids and gadgetry? Isn't an expenditure of $800 or $900 or more per year per child a rather expensive "socializing" service charge? What about the wishes of parents who send their children to school with the expectation and express desire that they will be taught to read?

In his book *Reading Without Dick and Jane,* Dr. Arthur S. Trace, Jr. states:

> From any point of view, the practice of teaching the rudiments of reading in the high school grades can in no sense be interpreted as an advance in the field of education; it is rather a giant step backward, and a tacit admission of a colossal failure of the present reading program. [3]

If children are being properly taught to read in the first grade — as every normal child should be, and many so-called "disadvantaged" children could be — why do we have a whole cadre of remedial reading and "special education" teachers across the country?

"And how do educators explain all the thousands and thousands of remedial reading cases?" [4] Flesch asks.

> To them, failure in reading is *never* caused by poor teaching . . .perish the thought. Reading failure is due to poor eyesight, or a nervous stomach, or poor posture, or heredity, or a

broken home, or undernourishment, or a wicked stepmother, or an Oedipus complex, or sibling rivalry, or. . . ." [5]

Professor Trace, who has "gone through many of the mountains of . . . 'studies' explaining why our children can't read," [6] has reached this conclusion:

Our reading experts are quite content with the notion that the United States has vastly more emotionally disturbed, half-blind, dimwitted, neurotic, malformed, maladjusted, under-nourished, glandularly deficient, and ill-treated children than any other country in the world. I am not prepared to accept that premise. There may be as many as 2 per cent or even 5 per cent of our children who for one good reason or another cannot learn to read well, but there are not 30 per cent or 50 per cent. . . . [7]

Have you ever heard a teacher say: "It's those paltry books we're using"? Or, "They didn't do a good job at college of teaching me how to teach reading"? Or, "There's nothing wrong with your little boy; a third of the children in this class are having trouble. There must be something wrong with our method of teaching"?

How often have you seen a report in your local newspaper stating the percentage of non-readers in your local tax-supported schools? Aren't you entitled to know? Shouldn't such information be made public?

Educator Glenn McCracken, one of the contributing authors in *Tomorrow's Illiterates* declared:

There is nothing wrong with American children today. They are the finest children this country has ever produced, because they have so many more advantages: better food and clothing, better health, better homes and schools, more communication and transportation facilities, and more of almost everything else than any other young people in history. If they don't learn to read it is the fault of the teaching, not the taught. [8]

Major factors which contribute to widespread quasi-illiteracy include: (1) wrong method, (2) poor textbooks, and (3) faulty teacher training. Let's take them one at a time.

(1) *Wrong method* often includes use of the "look-say" or "whole word" approach.

As Flesch mentioned, if you talk to your child's teacher about the matter, you're likely to hear something like this: "Oh, we do teach phonics." At that point pursue the issue a step further. Ask her at what age are children taught all the letters of the alphabet and all the speech sounds (e.g., *ch, oy, qu*). A smattering of phonics to quiet insistent parents will not get the job done.

As Flesch points out, "Systematic phonics is one thing, unsystematic phonics is another. . . . Phonics is something that a child can master completely, once and for all. . . ." [9]

Some educators will tell you there are various ways to teach children to read and phonics is only one of those ways.

There is no substitute for systematic phonics, just as there is no substitute for a key to the lock on the front door of your house.

In his recent book, *Who Pushed Humpty Dumpty? Dilemmas in American Education Today,* educator Donald Barr, referring to the reading program, Initial Teaching Alphabet (ITA), mentions "faddists [who are] ready to turn phonics into a gizmo." [10]

One program that I would classify as a distorted phonics approach came to my attention in 1971, when a mother expressed consternation about the content of her child's reading material. Too many of the "stories" had themes of the *bite, kick, hate,* or *hit* variety. (How does a six-year-old express violence?) Her child was having difficulty with spelling. *Eat* came out *et, cake* as *cak.*

The child's "take-home" papers offered a clue. Silent letters in some words were about half (some one-third) the height of other letters. The *a* in eat and the *e* in cake, for example, were de-emphasized. The silent letters in these words were not only comparatively small, but were blurred and hardly distinguishable.

A teacher admitted a transition period would be necessary before children learning by this method could read "normal" English.

(2) *Poor textbooks* are still in wide use. Unfortunately, even in some districts where phonics are taught, children may then be doomed to the old look-say-nothing type readers. If stories are dull and uninteresting, the child may develop a life-long distaste for reading. Children's readers which are deficient in moral and intellectual value are a tragic waste of children's time and taxpayer's money. Trace declares:

> No educators of any country have so thoroughly lost sight of
> the fact that while students are learning to read, they should be

reading something worthwhile. [11]

Apart from the fact that the selections in the Dick-and-Jane type readers make no consequential contribution whatsoever to the student's literary or scientific or historical or geographical education, they likewise make no consequential contribution to their patriotic education or to their moral education. [12]

Why can't students be "made aware of the greatness of their country's past, its inheritance, its heroes, its variety, and its beauty by reading about them in their readers"? [13]

In 1965, Trace charged: "Everything considered, the contents of the readers from which virtually all our children are obliged to learn to read are a national disgrace." [14] Better readers are available but vast numbers of children are still subjected to reading paltry content.

(3) *Faulty teacher training* cannot be overlooked when we examine the deficiencies of public education. Professor Charles C. Walcutt, in *Tomorrow's Illiterates* wrote:

One way to describe the reading problem is to say that it is a teacher problem and — even more — that it is a problem of the teaching of teachers. [15]

The sheer inertia of a machine involving professional reputations, course offerings in colleges and universities — indeed whole curricula in schools of education — and great financial investments in textbooks is tremendous. Add to these the psychological resistance of people who have been defending a system whose theory and justification they *do not themselves understand,* and you have perhaps identified the most important causes of our national plight. . . . [16]

Proficiency Standards

In 1971 the Arizona State Board of Education adopted a policy statement requesting performance levels in reading as a requisite to promotion. In addition, the statement provided that after 1974-75, high school graduates "shall . . . demonstrate ability to read at least at a ninth grade level of proficiency. . . ." [17]

Such efforts are not without resistance.

In Arizona, who do you suppose objected? An article in *The Phoenix Gazette* stated:

The AEA, which represents 16,000 teachers and administrators, said the reading policy is "a reversion to archaic, discredited and undemocratic educational practices dating back to the 19th century."

The AEA's objections to the policy are detailed in a five-page position paper which voices the fear that the policy ". . .will result in vastly increased numbers of school dropouts and 'pushouts'. . . . It will discriminate against children who come from disadvantaged environments and whose self-image, already negative in many cases, will only be made more so by their inability to meet predetermined reading performance levels."

Economically Disadvantaged Children

Much of the educational propaganda about the "socio-economically deprived" children would be almost laughable were these children not so often the victims of faulty analysis. I am firmly convinced that most "socio-economically deprived" children could and would learn to read in the lower grades if they were properly taught.

Let me tell you about a little girl I remember. She lived with her parents and a younger brother and sister in a small, three-room, weather-beaten house. There was no electricity, no running water, no central heat, no refrigerator. The unplumbed "bathroom" stood at the end of a path near the alley.

The family's furniture consisted of two beds, a small cupboard, a few straight chairs, a wooden table, and two stoves. The father was energetic and hard-working, but jobs were scarce. Income was spotty and varied from meager to zero. The father "plowed" a large piece of the yard with a spading fork, turning it into a garden, as a source of food.

The only book in the house was the Bible. There were no newspapers. There was no radio, no telephone, no car.

The little shack — which a kind landlord provided rent-free — was so dilapidated that after this family moved out, no one else lived there; the owner had it burned to the ground.

Yet, taught by her mother, this little girl learned to read, write, and spell many words at age five with nothing more than a pencil and paper. Her mother didn't have a college degree, nor a high school diploma, nor even an eighth grade certificate.

Don't tell me "socio-economically deprived" children need special curriculum or "special education" teachers because they are "culturally and educationally handicapped." I don't believe a word of it. I was that little girl. The year was 1930.

I see little, if any, correlation between a child's social or economic status and his potential for learning.

There are very probably thousands of prosperous, highly successful persons in these United States today who could tell you that poverty and even hunger not only did not hinder them from learning, but in some cases actually provided the motivation which prodded them toward later success and prosperity.

I'm not advocating poverty or malnutrition for anyone. But I consider the propaganda about the "disadvantaged" and "socio-economically deprived" children (blaming environment for "learning problems"), in most cases, as nothing but sheer malarky and a teacher cop out.

The child's home environment, frankly, is none of the teacher's business. It's high time teachers stop playing psychologist by analyzing "reasons" in the child's home environment as a scapegoat for their own inadequacies or for paltry textbooks or poor teaching methods. Elementary teachers should do what they are paid to do: teach children to read.

Some will say I have oversimplified the problem. I can only reply that for many years certain "experts" have overcomplicated the simple task of teaching children to read.

NOTES

1 Rudolf Flesch, *Why Johnny Can't Read and What You Can Do About It*, paperback ed., Perennial Library (New York: Harper & Row, Publishers, ©1955; first Perennial Library edition published 1966), p. 68 (hereafter cited as Flesch, *Why Johnny Can't Read*).

2 Albert J. Martin, "Achievement and Ability," Public Forum, *Coos Bay* (Ore.) *World*, May 5, 1971.

3 Arther S. Trace, Jr., *Reading Without Dick and Jane*, second printing (Chicago: Henry Regnery Company, 1965), p. 19 (hereafter cited as Trace, *Reading Without Dick and Jane*).

4 Flesch, *Why Johnny Can't Read*, p. 23.

5 *Ibid.*

6 Trace, *Reading Without Dick and Jane*, p. 27.

7 *Ibid.,* pp. 27, 28.

8 Glenn McCracken, *Tomorrow's Illiterates: The State of Reading Instruction Today,* Charles C. Walcutt, editor (Boston-Toronto: Atlantic Monthly Press published by Little, Brown and Company; ©1961 by Council for Basic Education, Washington, D.C.), p. 82.

9 Flesch, *Why Johnny Can't Read,* p. 108.

10 Donald Barr, *Who Pushed Humpty-Dumpty? Dilemmas in American Education Today* (New York: Atheneum, 1971; ©1958, 1960, 1961, 1962, 1963, 1964, 1966, 1967, 1968, 1969, 1971 by Donald Barr), p. 288.

11 Trace, *Reading Without Dick and Jane,* p. 151.

12 *Ibid.,* p. 144.

13 *Ibid.*

14 *Ibid.*

15 Charles C. Walcutt, ed., *Tomorrow's Illiterates: The State of Reading Instruction Today* (Boston-Toronto: Atlantic Monthly Press, published by Little, Brown and Company; ©1961 by Council for Basic Education, Washington, D.C.), p. 18.

16 *Ibid.,* p. 19.

17 "Arizona Takes a Step Forward," *Bulletin,* Council for Basic Education, Vol. 16, No. 2, October, 1971, p. 2, quoting from policy statement adopted by Arizona State Board of Education, July 26, 1971.

18 "Challenge Rejected," *The Phoenix Gazette,* August 24, 1971.

10

SOCIAL STUDIES FOR SOCIAL CHANGE

> Educationists profess to dispense with the remote past because of its alleged
> irrelevance to . . . [very recent] issues. The allegation is the hallmark of the New
> Ignorance.
>
> . . . Albert Lynd
> *Quackery in the Public Schools*

In 1972 in hundreds of American classrooms, school children — many
of them eleven- and twelve-year-olds — studied about such intriguing
things as the behavior of baboons and the mating urge of herring gulls. A
drawing in one booklet pictures the male gull atop the female. A
description is given of how the gulls communicate the mating urge.
Children are asked to compare gull communication to human communication.

The booklets on baboons and herring gulls are part of the social
studies course, *Man: A Course of Study* (M.A.C.O.S.). A number of
booklets replace the traditional textbook. Films, in color, are an
important part of the course. Games and records are also included.

One unit of the course deals with the lives and behavior of the distant
Netsilik Eskimos. One of the booklets is entitled *The Many Lives of
Kiviok.* (It might more appropriately have been called "The Many *Wives*
of Kiviok.") Kiviok takes wife after wife after wife — on occasion two at
a time. His wives are various kinds of animals in human form.

In one episode, his jealous mother-in-law kills her own daughter and
attempts to trick Kiviok into taking her for his wife. She does not
succeed, however, because he notices her weak, old legs. Kiviok mourns
for his murdered young wife — but eventually finds another.

The story of Netsilik mothers who deliberately permitted some of their
baby daughters to die at birth might offer children the "opportunity" to

consider the pros and cons of infanticide.

Then there is the story of the old Netsilik woman who was left alone to die on the ice. Should the old continue to live when they can no longer work and are a burden on the younger generation?

Are such profound topics appropriate for eleven- and twelve-year-olds? Is the seed-thought being planted that if you are not useful to society, it is all right — for the sake of survival of the group — to dispense with your life? Is such "education" a softening process for tolerance or acceptance by young American children of infanticide, euthanasia, senilicide? Or, if such is not the deliberate intent, will that be the result?

This is not to say that various cultures should not be studied objectively when the child is mature enough (when his own beliefs are fairly well established) to enable him to properly evaluate human behavior in other cultures. Even then, utmost care should be taken to make certain children are never left with the impression that evil in any form (any violation of God's laws) such as polygamy, infanticide, or senilicide is "right" in certain cultures, because persons in particular cultures consider it right. And children should never be led to believe there is no Absolute basis for morality.

True, no moral laws are embraced by all men everywhere. But there are Absolute Moral Laws applicable to all men everywhere, and by which all men everywhere shall one day be judged. Some things are wrong under all conditions, for all men everywhere — past, present, and future. Children should not be led to believe otherwise.

M.A.C.O.S. is supposed to help children discover what makes man human. The course proceeds on the underlying false assumption that man is an evolved animal. A M.A.C.O.S. brochure refers to "free-ranging baboons"[1] as "man's close primate relatives."[2] This absurd idea is in severe contradiction to the Biblical precept that man is a specially created being, made in God's own image, "a little lower than the angels." No animal was made in God's image.

Psychology professor Jerome Bruner (who was influential in the development of M.A.C.O.S.) stated, "We seek exercises and materials through which our pupils can learn wherein man is distinctive in his adaptation to the world, and wherein there is discernible continuity between him and his animal forbears."[3]

The fact is there is no "discernible continuity" between man and the animal kingdom because animals are not man's forbears.

The evolutionary idea is "utterly devoid of any genuine scientific basis." [4] Dr. Henry M. Morris, scientist, has declared. In the words of Dr. Morris:

> The false premise [upon which the idea of evolution is built] is the blasphemous assumption that man, who is a creature of God — a fallen creature at that — can explain God's creation without God and His revealed Word. . . . Like his father Adam, when he has rejected God's Word . . . [he] must explain everything in the universe, if he can, without reference to its Creator. [5]

Why should public schools use any social studies course which rests on belief in evolution, unless equal time is granted for another social studies course — for the same children — based on the Genesis account?

The Christian view is that "the solution given in the Bible answers the problem of the universe and man and nothing else does." [6]

Facts vs. Concepts

Teachers are admonished in one social studies book:

> Postulate, if you will, a child . . . subjected for twelve years to a "fact"-oriented, topic-centered course of social studies . . . . perhaps very little will be "true" as "fact" at the time of his leaving high school, twelve years later. His "school life" would, in a sense, have been "wasted." [7]

In the first place, who says the child needs to study "social studies" each year for twelve long years?

In the second place, anything that actually happened in the past is forever written in history; time cannot change it one iota. And if there's one thing youngsters need today, it's a little factual "stored" knowledge of their own heritage.

The child's twelve years will indeed have been wasted if he takes nothing with him when he graduates but an empty head and a skeptical, uncertain mind.

In addition to the fact that the predominate methodology (inquiry) of the New Social Studies is objectionable, the content of many of the books is also objectionable.

A total of twelve different series of the New Social Studies for grades one through six were examined in the early 1970's by textbook analyst, Mrs. Norma Gabler. Mrs. Gabler, who has gained nationwide publicity as a result of her fearless demands for better textbooks, says she cannot, as a Christian parent, recommend a single one of the twelve series of the New Social Studies she examined.

UNESCO

If we look back a few years, perhaps we could gain a better insight into today's problem. Soon after World War II, seminars were sponsored by UNESCO (United Nations Educational, Scientific, and Cultural Organization). A series of pamphlets for teachers entitled "Towards World Understanding" was published, following work at the seminars.

One of the pamphlets states, "The aim of this seminar is to formulate an educational programme leading to world-mindedness." [8] Writers of another of the pamphlets believed that before a child studies "national" geography, he should be "partly immunized against an exaggerated sense of the importance and beauty of his own country . . . against that error of perspective which is at the root of jingoism and nationalism." [9] The following statements also bear consideration:

> One of the chief aims of education today should be to prepare boys and girls to take an active part in the creation of a world society. . . .
>
> As an essential part of this preparation, pupils should learn about the United Nations and its Specialized Agencies, for it is the great contemporary effort . . . to move toward a world society. [10]
>
> As long as the child breathes the poisoned air of nationalism, education in world-mindedness can produce only rather precarious results. As we have pointed out, it is frequently the family that infects the child with extreme nationalism. [11]

"The study of history . . . raises problems of value which are better postponed until the pupil is freed from the nationalist prejudices. . . ." [12] This presumably is to be accomplished through "proper" teaching in the lower grades.

The schools are envisioned as the place to prepare the child through "a progression of loyalties" [13] to "enable him later to reach the climax of membership in the world community." [14] A "universal society" [15] is also the stated goal of the nontheistic religion of Secular Humanism.

It's my understanding that this subversive plan has never been officially adopted in public schools in the United States. Evidence strongly indicates, however, that various portions of the UNESCO plan, in many cases, have been incorporated.

Changing Loyalties

How are loyalties changed? "The changing of loyalty consists, in its primary step, of the eradication of existing loyalties." [16] This is the "unfreezing" process, which may prove effective with older children who have been "indoctrinated" by "narrow-minded" parents.

In his essay, *Life Without Prejudice*, the late Richard M. Weaver explained that an "unfixing of faith" [17] is necessary "to clear the ground." [18] An effective way to accomplish this is by causing people to "question the supports of whatever social order they enjoy, to encourage a growing dissatisfaction and a feeling that they have inherited a bad article." [19]

What better tool to accomplish this than "inquiry" — the predominate methodology of the New Social Studies?

This is not to say that problems should be ignored. But persistently harping on the "problems" of American society — past and present — while playing down or ignoring the abundant blessings of freedom under God, is conducive to promoting anything from frustrated dissatisfaction to anarchy. What are young children supposed to do about all these "problems" anyway?

The development of patriotism can be hindered by teaching young children "tolerance" of other cultures and other governmental systems while teaching them little about their own heritage and little about the advantages of free enterprise. Or, their own history, when taught, can be played down, distorted, or denigrated.

Many of our great American statesmen and heroes of past generations would have been at loggerheads with some of today's liberals and left-leaning planners.

How likely is it that Samuel Adams, in Boston in 1773, would have moaned, "How wasteful to have dumped all that tea into the harbor! We should have distributed it in the ghetto neighborhood!"

Can you visualize George Washington arranging a "summit meeting" with King George III and agreeing to maintain a "balance of power"?

Can you imagine General Douglas MacArthur declaring, "There is no substitute for co-existence"?

"No compromise" was their ultimatum.

For the young generation to have a thorough knowledge of their history obviously poses a threat to plans of utopian one-worlders. So what must be done? Rewrite history? Lose it in homogenized "social studies"? Discount it as "irrelevant"?

As Dr. Weldon P. Shofstall, State Superintendent of Public Education of Arizona, pointed out, the view that history is irrelevant "could be seriously held only by a person who consciously or unconsciously believes there are no permanent things of importance — no universal and eternal values." [20]

If factual history is not learned in the classroom (or elsewhere), continuity with the past is cut. Professor Thomas Molnar, in *The Future of Education,* wrote, "Only through the continuity of generations, their thinking and ideals, can a society provide for its own survival. [21] Tear out the root, and the plant will die." [22]

Emil Brunner said, "Uprootedness does not mean independence. On the contrary, the uprooted man can never become independent." [23]

Do you think social engineers sitting on high thrones of the educational hierarchy don't know this?

Guilt and Hate

Another possible means of uprooting loyalties to one's heritage is to give white youth a guilt complex because more than a hundred years ago some white Americans owned black slaves. Slavery, to be sure, is an unfortunate part of our history.

"It is obvious," however, as the late Manning Johnson wrote, "that placing the blame for all the Negroes' ills at the door of the white leaders in America is to remove all responsibility from the Negro. This tends to make the Negro:

    (a) feel sorry for himself;

    (b) blame others for his failures;

    (c) ignore the countless opportunities around him;

    (d) be jealous of the progress of other racial and national groups;

    (e) expect the white man to do everything for him;

    (f) look for easy and quick solutions as a substitute for the harsh realities of competitive struggle to get ahead.

"The result is a persecution complex — a warped belief that the white man's prejudices, the white man's system, the white man's government is responsible for everything . . . . the next logical step is hate. . . ." [24] Manning Johnson, incidently, was a Negro.

After old loyalties (such as patriotism) have been dislodged or uprooted, implanting new loyalties becomes easier.

The United Nations

Unfortunately, some have swallowed the fable that the United Nations is "man's last and best hope for peace." If this nation is to be blended into the One World they dream of, loyalties must "progress" toward a world governing power.

Numerous "rigid" minds of the older generation still remember World War II with its Pearl Harbor, its Bataan March, its Iwo Jima. They know something of the price of freedom, and consequently suffer from that "reprehensible" affliction called "patriotism."

The ideal place for one-worlders to spread their propaganda is in the classroom through textbooks and films.

How objectively have your children been taught about the United Nations?

Have they learned that nations contributing only five per cent of the budget and representing only ten per cent of the world's population can capture the two-thirds majority of votes required for action on important questions by the Assembly? [25]

Have they learned that tiny member-nations such as Equatorial Guinea with a total population of less than 300,000 — roughly the size of Akron, Ohio — have exactly the same voting power in the UN General Assembly as the entire United States? [26]

Have they learned that the United States kicked in 3.5 billion dollars between 1945 and 1970 to help finance the UN? And that those billions represented about one-third of the UN's entire regular budget [27] — while we retain only one vote out of 136 in the General Assembly?

Have they learned that "peace" in the Communist vocabulary means "to cease resistance to communism"? And that the UN deck is stacked with Communists and neo-Communists? Does this give new meaning to the cliché that the UN is "man's last and best hope for peace"?

Have they learned that the Communists have brought their special brand of peace to multitudes — by mercilessly slaughtering them —

(witness Hungary), since the inception of the UN?

Have they learned that Communist spies have used their official assignments as UN personnel as cover for their espionage activities in these United States? [28] That to provide aid and comfort to our enemies is treason? That to provide a base on our own soil from which spies can operate within our own borders does indeed bring aid and comfort to our enemies? Have your children learned that this alone is sufficient reason to remove the whole ungodly organization from our shores?

Fortunately, thanks to the work of various individuals and organizations around the country, some critical analysis of the UN is going on. Until the entire unsavory propaganda barrage promoting acceptance of the UN (particularly through public schools), is brought to a grinding halt, your children need not become indoctrinated.

The writers of Volume V of the "Towards World Understanding" series, concede: "The school can cultivate world-mindedness only if the parents support and continue the work, or in any case do nothing that runs counter to the intentions of the school." [29]

There is your answer. UNESCO-ites themselves have supplied it. The rest is up to you. You can teach your children some objective truth about the United Nations. You can teach them why our United States Constitution should never be made subservient to the UN Charter, the Universal Declaration of Human Rights, or any contrivance which would effectively destroy our national sovereignty. You can teach them that a humanistic one-world government would render freedom under God an impossibility. You can teach them the UN is an abysmal failure and is not "man's last and best hope for peace." Why? Because God has been left out.

Socialism

Social studies is the likely place socialism will be studied — whether objectively or otherwise. And certainly it should be studied objectively, whether it be the socialism of Red China, Soviet Russia, or the socialist programs in these United States.

Perhaps it's too much to expect our public education system to present an accurate, unbiased picture of socialism to children whose teachers' paychecks are drawn through a socialist plan. Not only are teachers paid via forcible taxation, but most children are required by law to attend state schools, where they are subjected to a state-selected or state-approved intellectual diet, whether or not their parents approve it. Is it surprising, then, to see other forms of socialism buttered over and presented to children as something good or desirable? Aren't we terribly inconsistent to teach children that socialism is "bad" in other countries (or are they ever taught that?) and then to present our own socialist programs as desirable or good? A former high school teacher would like to know:

> Where is the teacher who suggests that a good case might be drawn up for making social security voluntary rather than socialistically compulsory? Where is the teacher who brings his students to wonder how a government that competes with private enterprise can be expected to protect the rights of private enterprise? [30]

How many Americans, who are repelled at the thought of compulsory attendance of adults at political education classes in Red China, think nothing of sending their own children to compulsory classes in our public schools, where they may be indoctrinated in philosophies and ideologies antagonistic to both Christianity and freedom?

The New Social Studies based on inquiry (frequently beginning in the first grade) are among the most potentially dangerous textbooks ever used in American classrooms. I do not see how the use of such materials can fail to produce a generation of uncertain, frustrated children filled with cynicism and skepticism, if not agnosticism.

NOTES

1 *Man: A Course of Study,* brochure, 1973-74 Edition (Washington, D.C.: Curriculum Development Associates, Inc., ©1972), p. 2.

2 *Ibid.*

3 Jerome S. Bruner, *Toward a Theory of Instruction* (Cambridge, Massachusetts: The Belknap Press of Harvard University Press, ©1966 by the President and Fellows of Harvard College: the essay "Man: A Course of Study" appeared in different form in the *ESI Quarterly Report,* Spring-Summer, 1965), p. 74.

4 Henry M. Morris, *The Twilight of Evolution* (Grand Rapids, Michigan: Baker Book House, 1963), p. 14.

5 *Ibid.*

6 Francis A. Schaeffer, *The God Who Is There,* paperback ed. (Third American printing, Downers Grove, Ill.: Inter-Varsity Press, December, 1969, with permission from Hodder and Stoughton Limited, England; ©1968 by Francis A. Schaeffer), p. 111.

7 Center for the Study of Instruction, Paul F. Brandwein, et al., *Principles and Practices in the Teaching of the Social Sciences: Concepts and Values,* Blue-Level One (New York, Chicago, San Francisco, Atlanta, Dallas: Harcourt, Brace & World, Inc., ©1970), p. T-12.

8 *The Influence of Home and Community on Children Under Thirteen Years of Age: Towards World Understanding,* Vol. VI (Paris: United Nations Educational, Scientific and Cultural Organization, 1949), p. 37.

9 *In the Classroom With Children Under Thirteen Years of Age: Towards World Understanding,* Vol. V (Paris: United Nations Educational, Scientific and Cultural Organization, 1949), p. 12 (hereafter cited as *Towards World Understanding,* Vol. V).

10 *Some Suggestions on Teaching About the United Nations and Its Specialized Agencies: Towards World Understanding,* Vol. I (Paris: United Nations Educational, Scientific and Cultural Organization, 1949), p. 5.

11 *Towards World Understanding,* Vol. V, p. 58.

12 *Ibid.,* p. 11.

13 *Ibid.,* p. 8.

14 *Ibid.*

15 Fourteenth tenet, Humanist Manifesto I.

16 *Brain-Washing: A Synthesis of the Russian Textbook on Psychopolitics,* n.d., n.p. (distributed by Kenneth Goff, Englewood, Colorado), p. 20.

17 Richard M. Weaver, *Life Without Prejudice and Other Essays* (Chicago: Henry Regnery Company, 1965; the essay appeared in *Modern Age,* Summer, 1957), p. 2.

18 *Ibid.*

19 *Ibid.*

20 W.P. Shofstall, "The Trojan Horse In The Classroom," mimeographed paper, eighth ed., January 1, 1972, p. 7.

21 Thomas Molnar, *The Future of Education,* Revised Edition (New York, London: Fleet Academic Editions, Inc., ©1961, 1970), p. 30.

22 *Ibid.,* p. 152.

23 Emil Brunner, *Christianity and Civilisation,* Vol. II; Gifford Lectures delivered at the University of St. Andrews, 1948 (New York: Charles Scribner's Sons, 1949), pp. 33, 34.

24 Manning Johnson, *Color, Communism and Common Sense,* (New York: Alliance, Inc., 1958), pp. 43, 44.

25 Bruce W. Munn (UPI), "Great Decisions of 1970: U.N. Still Last, Best Hope for World Peace," *Roseburg* (Ore.) *News-Review,* March 25, 1970.

26 John C. Wetzel, *The United Nations — Myth vs. Reality: A Critical Look at the Record* (New Rochelle, New York: America's Future, Inc.; ©1970 by John C. Wetzel), p. 12.

27 *Ibid.,* p. 14; in 1972 the U.N. General Assembly approved a reduction to a ceiling assessment of twenty-five percent for any one member nation.

28 *Ibid.,* p. 3.

29 *Towards World Understanding,* Vol. V, p. 54.

30 A.R. Denison, "In Education It's Quality Not Quantity That Counts," *Roseburg* (Ore.) *News-Review,* May 21, 1969.

11

THE NEW ENGLISH — A REVOLT AGAINST RIGID RULES

It is ignorance, not knowledge, of grammar that chains a man's pen and his tongue.

> . . . Professor Arthur Bestoı
> *Good Housekeeping,* August, 1958

What is the "New English"?

"Generally speaking, an advocate of the New English is opposed to prescriptive grammar." [1] This means he is opposed to "grammar that lays down fairly definite rules and directions." [2] Traditional grammar sets down definite rules of "right and wrong" usage.

Promoters of the New English are likely to favor "appropriateness" over "correctness." The concern seems to be that rules are obstacles which may stand in the way. of the child's free flow of expression or "creativity."

As long as you can understand what the child means, what difference does it make whether or not his statements are grammatically "correct"? What difference does it make whether *anyone's* statements are grammatically "correct"?

If the child is ever to be taught correct grammatical usage, when is the best time to start?

Some advocates of the New English go so far as to maintain "that slum dialects are just as 'good' as standard English and should be considered socially acceptable." [3] Failure to overcome and replace slum dialect with correct grammar would hardly prepare slum children for gainful employment in later years in any field other than menial labor. Were incorrect grammar in its various forms, including slum dialect, to become "socially acceptable" in the business world, for example, we would have a debasing of the language.

Does it matter whether words are spelled correctly and periods are inserted in the right places — as long as the little darling is able to get his thoughts down unhampered? Yes, it does matter. Every time the child spells a word wrong — and there is a right way to spell most words — he's forming a habit. The more times that word is spelled wrong, and not marked or corrected — the deeper the error is ingrained. And, the longer the process of unlearning and relearning will take. Unfortunately, the child probably doesn't even know he has made an error. The same goes with incorrect usage and errors in punctuation. If errors are not unlearned, they can prove a detriment to him socially or economically in his adult life.

Authors of one elementary English book (teacher's edition) admit: "We have not attempted to make students proficient grammarians, for that is a lifetime's work." [4]

How often does a person's grammar improve after he leaves school? Don't most parents send their children to school to learn correct grammar, correct spelling, and correct punctuation, among other things? If children aren't going to learn essentials in the classroom, why send them at all?

Is it not strange we should have to plead the case for teaching children grammatical correctness with certain professors of English and those teachers they have influenced? How many of the professors promoting or defending the "New English" would have been able to obtain positions of prestige had they never learned the "rigid" standards of the grammatical correctness they discount? Why is their written propaganda promoting the "New English" meticulously correct in spelling, punctuation, and grammar?

In *Modern American Usage,* the late Wilson Follett commented, "If we go by what these men do instead of by what they say, we conclude that they all believe in conventional grammar, practice it against their own preaching, and continue to cultivate the elegance they despise in theory." [5]

An interesting story is told about Douglas MacArthur soon after he had taken command at West Point.

> One professor, a colonel, was furious at Doug's proposal to institute a rigorous two-year course in English. At a board meeting he interrupted MacArthur to denounce the idiocy of

wasting so much of a soldier's time teaching him how to handle words instead of weapons.

Doug endured the colonel's antediluvian prating as long as he could. . . . [Then] he roared, "Sit down, sir — *I* have the floor! I think your own impoverished speech proves my case for the need of an officer to learn how to present his views in an intelligent and convincing manner. Without this ability an officer may have the finest judgment in the world, he may even be as wise as Solomon, yet his influence will be practically negligible. We are not training military weapons at West Point, sir — we are training military *minds!* Without a solid grounding in English, no officer can either grasp or communicate the subtleties and complexities of international conflicts in the Twentieth Century. The pen, sir, is *still* mightier than the sword! [6]

A command of the English language is an invaluable aid to any American — whatever his line of work. How well have most young Americans mastered their native language?

The National Assessment of Educational Progress (NAEP) in recent years has conducted surveys in an attempt to assess learning achievement in various areas. Exercises in the mechanics of writing were given to 86,000 children in the nine, thirteen, and seventeen age groups and also to 8,000 young adults. In 1972, Dr. Henry Slotnick, (who prepared the report) was quoted in *The New York Times* as stating at a news conference, "Only four or five people in the whole assessment had a really good command of the English language." [7] *The New York Times* writer said Slotnick "meant that these writers were not limited to simple construction," [8] and that they were able to match "constructions and words precisely to the thoughts they wanted to convey." [9]

One with whom correctness (usage, punctuation, and spelling) is a habit has a distinct advantage over one who flounders in uncertainty, groping (against a habit of wrong usage) for the correct word, when the situation demands correctness.

Some or even many of the 86,000 children who took NAEP exercises may have studied traditional grammar rather than the "New English." If that was the case, can the New English improve the situation?

Why is the New English being promoted?

"Unquestionably the linguists have been motivated by a desire to apply the exact methods of scientific inquiry to the mystery of language, and they have seen traditional grammar as unreasonably rigid. . . ."[10] according to the coauthors of *A Consumer's Guide to Educational Innovations.*

Generally speaking, the advocate of the New English believes "there are no absolutes in language, all usage being relative. . . ."[11]

Such thinking goes hand-in-glove with the philosophy of gray thinking and situation ethics. If the philosophy of relativism (resulting from death of the absolutes) is to eat up Christianity and reign Supreme, it has to permeate every aspect of children's thinking.

How many parents on your street would endorse the New English if they understood it?

NOTES

1 Mortimer Smith, Richard Peck, and George Weber, *A Consumer's Guide to Educational Innovations* (Washington, D.C.: Council for Basic Education, 1972), p. 62 (hereafter cited as Smith, Peck, Weber, *Consumer's Guide*).

2 *Ibid.*

3 *Ibid.*

4 Richard Sanders, ed., Series Coordinator, Educational Development Corporation, *New Directions in English 1,* Teacher's Edition (New York, Evanston, London: Harper & Row, Publishers in association with Educational Development Corporation, Palo Alto, California, 1969), p. T-8.

5 Wilson Follett, *Modern American Usage,* edited and completed by Jacques Barzun, et al. (New York: Hill & Wang, Inc., 1966), p. 30.

6 Jules Archer, *Douglas MacArthur: Front-Line General,* Fourth printing, 1965 (New York: Julian Messner, Division of Pocket Books, Inc., © by Jules Archer 1965, 1963), pp. 62, 63.

7 William K. Stevens, "Survey Finds U.S. Youth Unskilled in Written English," *The New York Times,* February 3, 1972, p. C-23.

8 *Ibid.*

9 *Ibid.*

10 Smith, Peck, Weber, *Consumer's Guide,* p. 43.

11 *Ibid.,* p. 62.

12

MODERN LITERATURE — AVENUE TO CULTURE
OR CORRUPTION?

A particular train of thought persisted in, be it good or bad, cannot fail to produce its results on the character and circumstances.

. . . James Allen
As A Man Thinketh

A thistle seedling cannot break the soil and poke its head into the sunlight unless a thistle seed was first planted, either intentionally or by chance of nature. If more thistle seeds are scattered in your garden than vegetable seeds, you're likely to have more thistles crop up than vegetables.

The law of sowing and reaping, James Allen maintained, is just as certain in the mental realm as in the tangible realm of nature.

"As the plant springs from, and could not be without, the seed, so every act of a man springs from the hidden seeds of thought, and could not have appeared without them. This applies equally to those acts called 'spontaneous' and 'unpremeditated' as to those which are deliberately executed." [1]

Some would not agree with the latter statement and blame the "unpremeditated" act on some external factor. However, persistent or habitual thoughts help shape attitudes. The thoughts themselves may drop into the subconscious and lie forgotten while the attitudes they generated persist. Attitudes both reflect and affect disposition.

What happens when you habitually think depressing thoughts? You become depressed. When you think kind thoughts? You show kindness. When you think arrogant thoughts? You become haughty. When you fill your mind with sensual thoughts? You become lustful.

Character is "an individual's pattern of behavior." [2] What determines a person's pattern of behavior? His thinking.

If your pattern of thought is altered, sooner or later your pattern of behavior or character will reflect it. Almost 3,000 years ago, the writer of the book of Proverbs in the Bible wrote, "For as he thinketh in his heart, so is he." [3] What a person thinks about is vitally important. His persistent train of thought predicts what he is becoming.

This explains why parents should take time to look at some of the literature their children are reading in the classroom and to view some of the films their children are seeing.

It should be understood that the one undergoing change may be totally unaware his attitudes are being changed. He may even argue nothing *is* happening.

Novelist Isaac Bashevis Singer has said he often feels that "A lot of the evil taking place today . . . is the result of the rotten stuff this modern generation read in its school days." [4]

You would almost have to read some of the stories yourself to believe what is passing today in some public schools under the guise of literature. Much of it is sick — really sick. Themes include death, violence, rebellion, law-breaking, child-parent conflict.

Some of the books are slick-papered, beautifully bound. Many of the stories are vividly portrayed. Fascinating? Yes. Fascinating murder, sadism, suicide, blood, coffins, graves. Effective writing? Yes, indeed.

The fact that some of the stories are by well-known authors makes no difference. Literature must be judged by the message it carries and its potential for harm to those who read it.

A former high school English teacher had this to say about an eighth-grade literature book she examined:

> It had the most interesting stories I have ever read in any textbook, barring none. The only thing wrong was that four of the five stories I read would tend, I believe, to alienate children from their parents, downgrade policemen (cops), promote sadism, sympathize with cheaters and liars . . . [or might cause children to] think of God and Bible as negative. . . .
>
> Skeptics will say there has to be something good in the book. Naturally, If there wasn't no one would be fooled. . . . [5]

Perhaps the most dangerous books of all are those which intersperse the good with the bad. (If the books were one hundred per cent objectionable, their adoption and use in the first place would be less likely.)

I do not intend to suggest all literature used in the classrooms is bad. It isn't. But the inclusion of some good literature is not justification for use of the objectionable.

C. M. Ward declared, "A child is impressionable. That young life is easily stamped. . . . The soul of a child is as sensitive to impressions as a photographer's plate. Every influence registers. No one can argue against this." [6]

Do you think curriculum designers drawing up their "scope and sequence" and selecting six-year series of literature books don't know this?

"Oh," someone may say, "but I know those teachers. They're nice. They really are nice, and they're sincere."

Being nice and being sincere are not the criteria. You can be both nice and sincere and still be wrong. What kind of literature are teachers recommending or requiring your children to read?

Reality

A gimmick often used to defend the undesirable is to insist that it is reality.

One junior high principal, before a group of parents and taxpayers, attempted to defend the reading of profanity in an eighth grade classroom, by stating, "It's reality. They must learn to cope with it." Such thinking raises several questions:

Is this a life-adjustment class or an English class?

Are English teachers paid to teach children "to cope" with profanity or to teach them grammar?

Are school teachers, by recommending or requiring the reading of profanity, violating state laws?

Have state textbook commissions in some states set themselves above state laws by approving books containing profanity for use in public schools?

Haven't Supreme Court rulings in recent years made it quite clear that no child's religious rights shall be violated? For a Christian child to be required to read profanity, or listen to it being read, is a gross infringement upon his religious beliefs and his rights under the United States Constitution.

Speaking of reality, prostitution and marijuana are reality, too. By what method shall children be taught "to cope" with these "realities"?

There is some reality that has no place in the classroom.

Would you feed your children spoiled food for lunch because it is reality? Are their physical bodies more important than their minds and souls?

One mother said to me, "I want my children to read everything." Well, I don't — no more than I want him to eat everything. Just as his physical body depends to a large extent on what he eats, so his character will depend, to a large extent, on what he reads.

"My belief is that some literature fed to children in school would otherwise never be a part of the lives of the great majority, and deserves to be returned to its once isolated status of saner days." [7] This would surely include contemporary trash brought into the classroom wearing the respectable dress of "literature."

The genuine realist is one who values yesterday and tomorrow as well as today. The genuine realist acknowledges the unseen as well as the seen; he values the spiritual as well as the material; he acknowledges the eternal as well as the temporal.

Violence and Animalism

"Violence and animalism" are named as "the predominate characteristics of modern literature" [8] by Professor Duncan Williams in his analytical work, *Trousered Apes*. Not writing specifically of literature in public education, but of modern literature in general, he states, ". . .we are teaching savagery and are naively appalled at the success of our instruction." [9]

> Few, however, seem to recognize in this trend anything more than a purely literary or artistic phenomenon. It appears to be forgotten or ignored that literature and the arts in general are very real, formative, social forces, molding the face of the age while at the same time portraying it. [10]

Serious questions arise when violent and animalistic, profane and shoddy literature is brought into the classroom, and is either recommended or required reading for youngsters in their formative years.

When seed-thoughts of violence, murder, hate, and rebellion are planted and planted and planted in tender young minds and watered with the philosophy of relativism, we can hardly expect a crop of stable, respectable, kind, law-abiding young people.

What is the defense for violent, animalistic literature in the classrooms of America? What is the reason for so many selections in literature books with themes of hatred, sadism, death, blood, violence? Why so much emphasis on the generation gap — with a noticeable number of stories that portray adult or parent as villain and child as victim? Are such stories selected for the purpose of deliberate conditioning, intended to change children's attitudes? What kind of society are they trying to build?

I have been told that most textbook salesmen are former school teachers. Naturally they and their publishers will attempt to defend their source of income. But remember, in the final analysis, it's the buyer who controls the market. How long would publishers continue publishing such books if state textbook commissions flatly refused to adopt them? If local school boards refused to purchase them?

Unfortunately, local school boards too often rubberstamp whatever books are slid under their noses by persuasive curriculum administrators. Our crying need is for school board members who have at least as much concern for character-building textbook content as they have for figuring out ways to persuade wary taxpayers and parents to approve ballooned budgets.

"Oh well," someone argues, "the kids see violence all the time on TV anyway." Why not let them stay home and watch it on TV then? Why waste tax dollars and call it "education"? Conceding that many children do suffer undesirable mental intake from TV, does that justify giving them additional doses at school? And why should it be forced upon those children who reject garbage at home via the TV? And what about the rights of parents who object?

"What about the Bible?" someone asks. "Doesn't it contain lots of violence?" Yes, there are numerous accounts of violence in the Bible. The Bible gives many examples of man's evil nature. But it doesn't stop there. The Bible offers an answer to man's dilemma. The Bible points out man's need for Divine forgiveness and deliverance from his evil deeds. The Bible sets forth God's laws for man's behavior. The Bible teaches children to honor and obey their parents. The Bible commands parents to "provoke not" their children.

The Bible teaches an absolute concept of right and wrong. The Bible expresses God's love for mankind, offering forgiveness and eternal life through Christ to "whosoever will." The Bible offers hope (not despair), light (not darkness), peace (not frustration).

In contrast, what does much of the literature being read in countless public schools offer?

Existentialism

I mention nontheistic existentialism at this point for I wish the reader to draw a comparison between this breed of Humanism and the themes of some of the literature being read in many classrooms.

Existentialism "is a cult of nihilism and pessimism." [11] (Nihilism denies "the existence of any basis for knowledge or truth." [12] Nihilism also rejects "customary beliefs in morality, [and] religion," [13] including belief in eternal life.) Existentialism considers the universe purposeless and maintains that each man "as an individual . . . must oppose his hostile environment through the exercise of his free will." [14] Existentialism maintains that man should strive to "authenticate" himself while believing that physical death is the final end for him; hence, life is viewed as absurd.

Principal themes of existentialist literature include alienation, anxiety, nostalgia, homelessness, nausea, despair, absurdity, and death.

Surely any literature which leads its reader into dark chasms of despair and despondency is wrong. What happens to the youth who reads such literature and is left with feelings of hopelessness, alienation, or despair?

What can morbid literature contribute to mental health? Isn't it a little strange at a time when mental health is a matter of concern that educators will attempt to defend violent, morbid literature?

A high school principal emotionally pleaded with his local school board for more counselors. He felt they might help prevent some student from committing suicide. One mother wryly remarked later, "If they'd get rid of those literature books, maybe they wouldn't need so many counselors."

It is estimated that at least 1,000 college students in the United States commit suicide each year (and thousands more attempt it). While various factors contribute, one overwhelming thought for many of these poor, despairing souls swallows up all else: Life is meaningless. A study at one university found that more suicides occurred among English majors than any other group. [15]

Apart from God man *is* in despair. Man *is* adrift. Man *is* lost and alienated — not only from his Creator-God, but also from himself. This is true because he is in rebellion against the One in whose Image he is made.

Do public school teachers have the right to lead children's minds down despair-filled paths without letting them know there is a way out of the dark chasm? That man need not remain in despair, in alienation?

When children are required to read existentialist literature, is it so-labelled? Are they told that existentialism is one breed of Humanism? That Humanism is a religion whose followers reject belief in the Creator-God and in life-after-death?

The Bible As Literature

In recent years some schools have implemented classes entitled "The Bible As Literature." Some believe such a course will balance the use of existentialist literature, but it couldn't possibly do that unless all children study the "Bible as Literature" on an equal time basis with humanistic literature. How many children are required to take a course in the "Bible as Literature"? In contrast, how many children are now required to read existentialist literature — often unlabelled as such?

Furthermore, some serious questions need to be answered regarding "Bible as Literature" classes in public schools. Is the Bible being presented as Absolute Truth, inerrant, Divinely inspired? Or as just another book? As myth? As a legend? As secular history? As secular literature?

What are children told about the Genesis account of creation? About the Virgin Birth? About miracles Jesus performed? About Jesus' resurrection? About His Ascension?

Are children being led to believe Jesus was a good man, a great teacher, but not the Divine Son of God? Such a belief is not Christianity; it is Humanism.

From time to time articles appear, particularly in religious journals, proclaiming "Bible as Literature" classes are being implemented in public high schools. Many gullible, naive Christians do doubt rejoice when they read such articles. In some cases the classes may be worthwhile and beneficial; however, such classes *prima facie* should never be assumed to be acceptable.

Such a class may go so far as to include the blasphemous rock opera

"Jesus Christ Superstar," which *Newsweek* quoted one young person as describing this way:

> They turn the whole thing around to where Judas was really a good guy and Jesus was bad. They make a mockery of the Gospel, the Crucifixion, the Blood, the Son of God and the price paid for sins. . . . It made me sick . . . when I read the text. [16]

A writer in the *English Journal* [17] points out there is a difference between teaching the Bible *as* literature and the Bible *in* literature. He gives an example of an allusion to the Bible *in* literature:

> In *To Kill a Mockingbird* young Scout hears her father and uncle discussing her father's decision to defend a Negro charged with rape in the bigoted southern town of Maycomb. [18]

The writer then quotes a passage from *To Kill a Mockingbird,* and comments:

> Without knowledge of the Bible the student understands that this was an unpleasant decision, but he may miss the agony. With the background of the Garden of Gethsemane he understands Atticus Finch's acceptance that he will be crucified by the town, that he has to drink the bitter cup alone, and that he must do it to save the souls of his children. . . . [19]

To the genuine Christian is such an allusion acceptable?

The writer, in the same article, gives another example. He quotes Melville in *Typee* and then states:

> Again the uninformed student might understand that the natives have a life of ease. But Melville has an ax to grind. He talks of Typee as a Garden of Eden in which the natives are as innocent as Adam and Eve before they sinned. It is part of Melville's purpose to show that these people were corrupted not by their inheritance of the Original Sin nor through their own depraved acts but by the Christians — even the missionaries — who brought civilization to the islands. His use of the biblical allusion reinforces . . . his point and subtly replaces the outright attack ·on the church that his publisher made him delete from his manuscript. [20]

This should give some insight as to what can be done with the Bible in literature. Literature has, of course, been used for centuries as a tool by writers with a philosophy to promote or an ax to grind. It is not difficult to see that literature could also be used advantageously by teachers with a philosophy to promote or an ax to grind.

We can conclude, then, that the study of the Bible as literature, or allusions to the Bible in literature, can be helpful or harmful depending upon who teaches the class, what materials are used, and how the materials are handled.

NOTES

1 James Allen, *As A Man Thinketh* (Fleming H. Revell Company, n.d.), pp. 9, 10.

2 *Webster's New World Dictionary of the American Language,* Encyclopedic Edition, s.v. "character."

3 Prov. 23:7a.

4 Isaac Bashevis Singer, "Writing for Kids," *The Open Court Newsletter* (Open Court Publishing Company, La Salle, Illinois), Vol. VII, No. 3, January, 1973, (article reprinted by Open Court "through the Courtesy of Publishers-Hall Syndicate"), p. 3.

5 A.R. Denison, "Textbook Taken to Task by Sutherlin Man," *Roseburg* (Ore.) *News-Review,* October 27, 1969.

6 C.M. Ward, "Environment," (Revivaltime Radio sermon), March 21, 1971.

7 A.R. Denison, "Great Majority Has No Need for Questionable Literature," *Roseburg* (Ore.) *News-Review,* August 12, 1969.

8 Duncan Williams, *Trousered Apes* (New Rochelle, New York: Arlington House, 1972; previous ed. Churchill Press Limited, England 1971), p. 35, American Edition.

9 *Ibid.,* p. 29.

10 *Ibid.,* p. 30.

11 *Webster's New World Dictionary of the American Language,* Encyclopedic Edition, s.v. "existentialism."

12 *Ibid.,* s.v. "nihilism."

13 *Ibid.,*

14 *Ibid.,* "existentialism."

15 "Life and Literature," *Emphasis,* September 1, 1970, p. 7.

16 *Newsweek,* Vol. LXXVIII, No. 17, October 25, 1971, p. 84.

17 Thayer S. Warshaw, "Teaching the Bible As Literature," *English Journal,* Vol. 58, No. 4, April, 1969, p. 571; the *English Journal* is "The Official Journal

of the Secondary Section of National Council of Teachers of English."
18 *Ibid.*, pp. 571, 572.
19 *Ibid.*, p. 572.
20 *Ibid.*

13

IS THE NEW MATH A BIG MISTAKE?

Mathematics is an expression of the orderly nature of the created universe and conforms to the created order of God.

... T. Robert Ingram

In the Fall of 1972 a man with a doctorate in chemistry took his child's fourth-grade math book to the office where he worked. He and others (some with advanced degrees) flunked the "test" they gave themselves, comprised of fourth-grade problems. That particular book, he said, "is so vague and abstruse as to defy rational thought." [1]

The book is part of a series said to be one of the two biggest sellers in this country.

Many parents in recent years have experienced the frustration of trying to help their children understand the "New Math" and have pondered its value. After a decade of widespread use, studies revealing comparative test scores with traditional math are beginning to confirm what many parents suspected all along.

"There *is* considerable evidence of the decline in computational skills connected with the use of the new math. . . ." a writer in the March, 1973, *Bulletin* of the Council for Basic Education, stated.

A study in a northeastern state indicated that students taught the New Math fell an average of two grade levels behind children taught conventional math. [2]

"A similar study of California grade schoolers found that those taught standard 'rithmetic ten years ago scored twice as high on a nationwide test as the current crop raised on new math." [3]

In defense of the New Math, John J. Sullivan, (Associate, Bureau of Mathematics Education, State Education Department, Albany, New York), maintains, "It is unfair to judge the 'New Math' on the basis of how well students compute. The 'New Math' does not strive for exceptional computational proficiency." [4]

Which is more important for the majority of children — the New Math or computational skills? Or, should both be taught? Should the New Math be taught before computational skills are mastered?

Good learning moves from the known to the unknown, from the simple to the complex. Should broad concepts be taught before, or along with simple combinations?

One of the more common defenses of the New Math seems to be that many teachers don't know how to teach it. This may be true, but it really misses the point. Even if all elementary teachers did know how to teach it, should it be taught to elementary children? To all children?

Jacob Landers, (Assistant Superintendent of New York City Schools), pinpointed the issue when he interpreted Professor Morris Kline, (author of *Why Johnny Can't Add*), as asking, essentially this:

> Should one teach etymology before reading and writing? Teach bone structure and mechanics before teaching children how to walk? Teach the bases of other number systems to children who don't understand our own number system (using teachers who are often equally ignorant of the decimal system)? Teach set theory and nomenclature to children who can't add and subtract simple numbers? [5]

Some well-qualified mathematicians believe the New Math should not be taught at all in the elementary grades. Every child of normal intelligence should be taught computational skills (arithmetic) in the lower grades. But the New Math is not for every child — not even in high school — just as shorthand or sewing or learning to repair a light cord is not for every child. When taught, the New Math should follow a solid foundation of computational skills.

Some have posed the thought that the New Math might be a deliberate attack on the competence of the young generation's ability to think straight. Certainly that is not the intent of the vast majority of teachers. But the New Math could well contribute to that result, whether intentionally or unintentionally.

One educator, T. Robert Ingram, has said, "The 'New Math' is a *tour de force* supposed to demonstrate that even mathematics is a relative science. . . ." [6] He believes, "This movement is dedicated to proving there is no such thing as 'truth' (unchanging reality)." [7]

For many children the New Math is too complex, too complicated. Subjecting a child daily to problems which cause him confusion, frustration, uncertainty, and anxiety cannot contribute much to his "mental health."

Widespread use of the New Math should remove all doubt that curriculum in many districts of our nation's public school system (and consequently the thinking of large numbers of the next generation) can be manipulated by a small clique of non-elected persons. Such will be the case as long as school board members succumb to pressure or merely act as rubberstamps. This is true, not only of the New Math, but also of the inquiry-oriented New Social Studies, the New English, and virtually every other area of modern public education.

Millions of children in the last ten years have been victims of this blundering experiment of innovators and promotors of the New Math — not to mention millions of wasted tax dollars.

There are straws in the wind that indicate the New Math may be on its way down, if not out. Declining test scores of students can no longer be ignored. Some state boards are beginning to de-emphasize the New Math and write new guidelines with more emphasis on computational skills. This is particularly necessary at elementary levels.

Traditional math had its defects, especially when poorly taught. But it also had value. Memorization of multiplication tables or addition through rote and drill alone, without understanding, can be vexing and frustrating for a child. It's the teacher's responsibility to see that arithmetic is taught in such a manner the child understands the process and the need and is motivated to learn.

If properly taught, mathematics (including arithmetic) should help develop children's ability to think logically.

NOTES

1 Jay Mathews (LA Times-Washington Post Service), "Parent Fails, Flails New Math Lesson for Grade Schools," (Portland) *Oregonian,* November 23, 1972.

2 *National Review,* July 6, 1973, p. 719.

3 *Ibid.*

4 *Bulletin,* Council for Basic Education, Vol. 17, No. 9, May, 1973, p. 8.

5 Jacob Landers, *Bulletin,* Council for Basic Education, Vol. 17, No. 9, May, 1973, p. 10.

6 T. Robert Ingram, "The New Math and Twisted Minds," mimeographed paper T-76, (distributed by the Mel Gablers, Longview, Texas).

7 *Ibid.*

14

SEX EDUCATION FOR THE NOW GENERATION

The pathway of history is littered with the bones of dead civilizations and fallen empires. Most of them had rotted out before the barbarians battered down the gates. They had rotted out with corruption and dishonesty and the search for kicks.

. . . Jenkin Lloyd Jones
Editor and Publisher, *Tulsa Tribune*

Whatever else heated sex education battles across the country in recent years accomplished, they caused many parents to take a second look at the schools their children attend.

I have yet to meet the parent who is opposed to sex education for his or her children. All of us at a particular time in our lives need factual information regarding reproduction and sex. No one objects to that.

What many parents do object to is having the schools usurp a God-given right and responsibility that is, and should be, a personal matter between parents and their children. Many parents resent the insult, implied or spoken, that "parents aren't qualified," which in many cases, is a false accusation.

Referring to second-graders, a teacher asks, "Why should I teach them how their feet, their eyes, their ears, their muscles work, but not teach them about *that*?"

I'll tell you why. Their feet, their eyes, their ears, per se, have nothing to do with morals. Sex does. Many parents believe sex education should never be taught without an absolute standard of morality. If this is their religious belief — and for many it is — then the school has no right whatever to infringe upon the constitutional religious rights of parents whose children are involved.

Many parents do not wish their teen-agers to be presented information on sexual perversions of various kinds in a manner which indicates that such deviation is right or normal and is simply an "alternative" to normal husband-wife relationships. Such teaching clearly violates the rights of parents who believe that homosexuality, for example, is morally wrong.

Christians are sometimes falsely accused of believing sex is evil or "dirty." The Christian recognizes God as the Creator of the natural world and mankind. Sex is part of God's design. God looked at man and saw that he was lonely. In His infinite wisdom and mercy He created for him a helpmate. He didn't give Adam another man for a companion; he gave him a woman. God looked at His creation and saw that it was good. What God has called good, the Christian does not call evil. The Christian accepts sex as a valued, sacred trust. He esteems it more highly than those who consider themselves no more than evolved animals.

There's a vast difference between a thing being evil and it being personal. It's just as distasteful to discuss intimate details of sex publicly (including public school classrooms) as it is to discuss the details of one's financial affairs or to describe one's physical ailments at a public meeting. It's an insult to the sensibilities of refined people.

Many parents object, and rightfully so, to children discussing sensitive and personal matters in mixed classes, because this may result in breaking down their children's modesty. "There is something brutish . . . and unholy about boys and girls talking about sex organs and sex intercourse like they were common items in a five and dime store." [1]

Some educators will argue that giving teen-agers all the "facts" will quell their curiosity and lessen the likelihood of experimenting. "However, sexual desires like physical hunger are . . . natural emotions, and you do not get rid of hunger pains in your stomach by reading all about the different kinds of foods and having pictures of seven-course meals flashed before your eyes. The more you see pictures of food and the more you think of food, the hungrier you become." [2]

Aren't the teen years difficult enough without the schools compounding the problem? Does anyone really believe that putting outhouse-type graffiti on blackboards, asking children to define the meaning of uncouth four-letter words, and teaching methods of contraception in the classroom will decrease venereal disease or lower the illegitimate birth rate?

Remember this:

> Whatever gets your attention gets you. . . . Whatever you hold within the mind tends to pass straight into act. Ideas are not passive; they are active. . . . Ideas held within the mind are destiny. . . . "Never *think how,*" for if you *think how* you will soon *plan how.* [3]

In 1971, four years after the New York City school board inaugurated "Family Life" education, including sex education (elementary grades through high school), the label "cyesis" was chosen for six special schools. "Cyesis" means pregnancy. The schools were needed to take care of more than 1,700 pregnant girls in grades seven through twelve. Another 1,200 pregnant girls were expected to continue attending classes in their regular schools. In addition, an estimated 50,000 girls had obtained legal abortions in the previous year-and-a-half. What went wrong? Some educators thought the program wasn't sufficiently implemented. Some students claimed they needed more information about sexuality and the prevention of pregnancy. [4]

Obviously the crying need was not for more education on *sexuality* but on *morality.*

And how likely is it that public schools would teach the Christian ethic — premarital sexual abstinence — when many educators view man as an animal, the product of evolution? Animals have no restraints, no morals. As an evolved animal, man has no obligation to obey God's laws (if God does indeed exist). Man's morals then are man-made and man's responsibilitity is to himself and to his fellow "animals." So what's wrong with premarital sex — as long as the "animals" are "responsible" to one another?

Does this explain, at least in part, the emphasis in recent years in public education on the Fourth "R" — Responsibility? What would the fourth "R" mean in this sense? Responsible enough to use contraceptives? Responsible enough to go to the county health facility or doctor's office if V.D. symptoms appear? Responsible enough to pay for an abortion if contraception fails?

Some educators cite the soaring epidemic of venereal disease and the many unwed pregnant girls as the reason for trying to get sex education into the schools. Ironically, out of the other side of their mouths, they tell us information on venereal disease must not be taught as part of sex education, but with "Diseases." (The fear of "catching" a disease might interfere with the little darlings' spontaneity.)

Which brings us to the next question: Who delegated the solving of social problems to educators?

If their record for the past few decades of teaching children to read, spell, and add is any criterion, we certainly shouldn't burden them further with additional social tasks. Or, since man is a "social animal," is teaching children sexology more important than teaching them to read and write and add? Some, no doubt, would say it is.

The New Morality Cult and the Intellectual Descendants of Darwin may insist that sex relations—even for unwed teen-agers—are necessary for health reasons, or at any rate are not wrong. The "need" then would be to make sex "safe" and enjoyable (without inhibition or guilt feelings, without danger of pregnancy or venereal disease) for the teen-ager. And the way to meet this "need," obviously, is with sex education, i.e., graphic descriptions, methods of contraception, etc., as distinguished from so-called plumbing courses: menstruation and reproduction.

So what is the answer? Should schools dispense birth control pills to girls and protective devices to boys? Why shouldn't teen-agers shed "Puritanical" inhibitions and strive to reach their "full potential"?

Does such a way of life release tensions and contribute to physical and mental health?

> Pagan psychiatrists, seeing people struggling with sex on the level of law and duty and ending in a frustration and a conflict, and knowing nothing of the possibilities of grace, [the Grace of God] advise people to go out and find "your man" or "your woman," regardless. What happens? . . .Has it cured the conflict? It has precipitated a worse conflict. . . . No more dangerous idea has been dropped into the soul of the sexually chaotic to make them more chaotic. . . . One of the reasons why this age is very sex-conscious and increasingly neurotic is this teaching. [5]

It has been said that the person who is sexually well-adjusted doesn't have sex on his mind every waking moment. By that criterion, where does this leave the sexologists — who aren't content to take care of only their own sexual problems, but apparently see themselves as "ministers" to the sexually frustrated? In that capacity, they can think and talk about it all day, every "working" day, week after week, month after month, year after year, ad nauseam.

And how "normal" are teachers who are eager beavers to teach sex education classes?

Which is the more normal, well-adjusted person — the average Christian or the average sexologist?

I doubt that Christians in our own generation have, or in the previous centuries had, the serious sexual maladjustments or "Puritanical" inhibitions that certain modern sexologists accuse them of.

One false accusation sometimes thrown at Christianity is that the Christian religion holds the sole purpose of sexual relations to be reproduction. Such a charge cannot be documented in Scripture.

Is the downgrading and berating of Christian morality by the antagonistic sexologist really symptomatic of a deep-seated problem in his own soul? Does he hurl his venomous darts at the religion of Christians because he has an ax to grind with God, Who wrote some Absolute Rules regarding sex?

In the United States in recent years, "Puritanical" inhibitions have hit an all-time low. And almost simultaneously our divorce rate has hit an all-time high. What is the answer?

> When sex is found in God, then sex finds itself fulfilled. One man and one woman live together in moral faithfulness, a home is set up, children come, love is the bond. That is sex fulfilled and sex beautiful and beautifying. Then sex is "yours." But suppose you listen to this lie: "It shall be yours, take it, for it belongs to you apart from morality and apart from God." What happens? Is sex "yours?" No, you do not have sex, sex has you. It dominates your thinking, your acting, you. You become its slave. [6]

Whether or not educators agree with the Christian standard, one fact remains: In sex education, as in other areas of curriculum, the Constitutional religious rights of Christian parents and children still hang heavy over their heads.

Venereal Disease Education

It's probably correct to say that venereal disease education is now being taught in many public schools, and has been for several years. And where this is the case, has venereal disease increased or decreased among teen-agers? *What* is being taught?

Are students being taught they can be infected with gonorrhea and show no immediate, external symptoms?

Have they been taught that serious complications from syphilis "sometimes develop before the individual is aware he is infected"? [7] That "twenty or more years after the disease (syphilis) is contracted, it may strike down its victim with a dreaded or fatal complication"? [8] That "one late manifestation of syphilis is paresis, an insanity caused by syphilis hitting the brain cells"? [9]

Have they been taught that "syphilis not only attacks the brain, causing insanity, and the spinal cord, causing the excruciating pains of locomotor ataxia, but it frequently attacks the heart"? [10]

Are these "qualified" educators telling teen-agers that "syphilis is . . . the cause for many a baby born macerated and dead"? [11] That "if an infected baby lives, it may have various physical or mental deficiencies"? [12] That "not only do these handicapped children have to pay a price during their lives, but their parents, as they look daily on their deformed or insane children, must pay dearly and bitterly with lifelong remorse"? [13]

Have they been told that "when the mother is infected with gonorrhea, the eyes of the baby can become infected as it passes through the birth canal" [14] and that, in the absence of immediate medical precautionary measures, lifelong blindness is a likely result?

Do they know that the incidence of gonorrhea among girls taking the pill may be as much as three times that of the national average — if the same holds true in the United States as a doctor's study in England indicated? [15] And that, if this be true, girls on the pill are more likely to be carriers, than those not taking it?

Are boys being told that because there is no "simple, reliable blood test for detecting gonorrhea," [16] males with no external symptoms (who believe they have been exposed) — in order to find out whether or not they have been infected — "must endure having a thin metal wire inserted in the urethra to scrape a cell sample from the mucous membranes"? [17]

In short, are educators bringing children to see the seriousness, the possible dreadful consequences of venereal disease — or are they leading children to believe it is just a temporary, unfortunate discomfort of little more importance than a cold — something one trip to the doctor can cure?

Are educators encouraging children to use protective devices? If so, are they thereby encouraging promiscuity?

What have your children been taught about venereal disease in the classroom? Ask them.

And whatever else they have or haven't been told, be sure they know about God's plan: That two — and only two — (of opposite sexes) should be faithful to each other, exclusively, as long as they both shall live. God's plan, when complied with completely, is "so effective in the prevention of the vast complications of horrible venereal diseases, that again we are forced to recognize another medical evidence of the inspiration of the Bible." [18]

NOTES

1 David Webber, "A Critical Study of Sex Education in the Public School System," (mimeographed paper), pp. 12, 13.

2 *Ibid.,* p. 7.

3 E. Stanley Jones, *The Way* (New York-Nashville: Abingdon-Cokesbury Press; © MCMXLVI by Stone & Pierce), p. 146; Jones' use of "Never think how" is a quotation from Rom. 13:14, Moffatt.

4 "Trouble in River City," ("Journal After the Fact"), *The American School Board Journal,* Vol. 159, No. 6, December, 1971, p. 5.

5 E. Stanley Jones, *The Way to Power and Poise* (New York-Nashville: Abingdon-Cokesbury Press; © MCMXLIX by Pierce & Smith), p. 254.

6 *Ibid.*

7 S.I. McMillen, M.D., *None of These Diseases,* Twelfth printing, May, 1972, (a Spire book published by Pyramid Publications for Fleming H. Revell Company, © MCMLXIII by Fleming H. Revell Company), p. 42 (hereafter cited as McMillen, *None of These Diseases*).

8 *Ibid.*

9 *Ibid.*

10 *Ibid.,* p. 44.

11 *Ibid.,* p. 39.

12 *Ibid.*

13 *Ibid.*

14 *Ibid.,* p. 38.

15 "The Pill and the Plague," *Life Messengers,* December, 1971.

16 "Invisible Gonorrhea," *Newsweek,* Vol. LXXX, No. 15, October 9, 1972, p. 97.

17 *Ibid.*

18 McMillen, *None of These Diseases,* p. 45.

15

PPBS — THEIR PROGRAM IS TO PROGRAM

Single acts of tyranny may be ascribed to the accidental opinion of a day; but a series of oppressions, begun at a distinguished period, and pursued unalterably . . . too plainly prove a deliberate systematical plan of reducing us to slavery.

. . . Thomas Jefferson

The letters PPBS stand for Planning, Programming, Budgeting System. Broadly speaking PPBS is a formula. [1] We're going to consider PPBS as it pertains to education, although that is only part of the total picture. (PPBS has been introduced into various governmental agencies and certain large corporations.)

PPBS is, in part, a computerized budgeting system. Its potential, however, extends far beyond use as a sophisticated bookkeeping system.

Accountability is the key word for PPBS as it applies to education. This can mean far more than that the teacher shall be held accountable for your child learning to read, write, and add. It is unlikely anyone would object to that.

As noted earlier, education has been redefined. Traditionally, learning meant the acquisition of factual knowledge. The new goal is to change the behavior of the student.

Through PPBS, teachers can be held accountable for specified objectives which may include changing the child's attitudes, beliefs, and behavior in a predetermined direction.

This change can be brought about through implementation of various techniques considered in previous chapters such as inquiry method, sensitivity training and positive reinforcement. Selective use of tapes, films, and textbooks can aid the process of planned change in the child's attitudes, beliefs, and behavior. The child may then be tested or observed in the affective (attitude, belief, emotional) domain as well as

113

the cognitive (academic knowledge) domain, and the results computerized and stored in data banks.

If the child does not meet predetermined goals, he can be "recycled" until the change occurs. Thus the teacher becomes "accountable" to the state for "changed behavior" of her students. If a particular teacher has too many students who require frequent recycling, that teacher may need recycling. If she refuses to "cooperate" or will not "produce," she may be dispensed with as "incompetent" or "insubordinate."

I am indebted to Mrs. Deloris Feak, of California, for the following summary, taken from one of her speeches, explaining the four primary phases of PPBS:

(1) [Planning or] determining the "product" we want to create, then designing material that will accomplish the task. It consists of goals, objectives, concepts, and the necessary supportive material. . . . [This] includes the new teaching methodologies of Conceptual Inquiry, Sensitivity Training, Psycho-drama as role playing, to name a few.

(2) "Programming" — this is the transmission belt of the system. It consists of seeing that the concepts . . . are incorporated all down the line—*accepted and implemented!*. . . .

(3) The third step is increased and constant evaluation, or data collecting, on the student and those who affect him, to determine if the goals and objectives . . . are being met; . . .*is* the "product" which they set about to create actually coming into being?. . .

(4) The fourth step is "recycling;" this concerns modification of input. If the current "input" (meaning pertinent and necessary indoctrination *materials, methods* and cooperative *personnel*) are not achieving the desired results, then modifications will have to be undertaken. . . . [2]

Mrs. Feak further explains:

We are talking about creation of a product — we are envisioning the "product," we are preparing to put into motion the necessary planning, programming, and budgeting to create that product. And in this case, we are talking about human beings as the "product" about to be created via this computerized system. This is, indeed, the plan for "creation of the new man," and . . . everyone connected with his development along this "creation" route is a "variable" . . . especially his teachers. . . . The state is going to make them "accountable" for delivering the product — that "product" being the . . . student that the state has planned, programmed, and budgeted for.

This term "accountability" is the connotation word for PPBS — again, it has a nice sound, and everyone thinks it means what he wants it to mean. . . . What they [teachers] never seemed to realize before was that leading and encouraging young children in "open-end" discussions, "rap sessions" and other sensitivity training techniques such as role-playing, was also an invasion of the children's and their families' privacy. [3] So, while we sympathize [with teachers] . . . in that they are now being "evaluated" by the same system that "conned" them into performing "evaluations" of their students and their families, we would also ask them to develop some spine. . . . [4]

Like the students they are guilty of manipulating, teachers, by cooperating with such schemes, themselves become "the shadows, the echoes, the tools of other men." [5]

Citizen committees are a very important part of the process of implementing change. Mrs. Mary Thompson, who lectures on PPBS, believes these committees "are always either self-appointed or chosen, never elected. They always include guidance from some trained 'change agents' who may be administrators, curriculum personnel or local citizens." [6]

The well-meaning citizens serving on such committees are, in many cases, just dupes, used to help achieve predetermined goals. Mrs. Thompson continues:

The ingeniousness of the process is that everybody thinks he is having a voice in the direction of public schools. Not so. . . . The change agents at the district level then function to "identify" needs and problems for change as they have been programmed to identify them at the training sessions. . . . This is why the goals are essentially the same in school districts across the country. [7]

"Community involvement" is encouraged; "input" by constituents of the district is welcomed at public hearings. Why? Identifying the opposition is important to facilitating change. Mrs. Thompson says, "Data gathering is not to find out what *you* want, it is to find out where you are . . . [and] what you think. . . ."[8] These public hearings help change agents to identify "the nature and scope of resistance to programs and [to decide] how best to circumvent resistance."[9]

Reports from these "citizens committees" are eventually presented to school boards, who, after having agreed to delegate their duties to the "advisory committee" in the first place, can hardly do less than rubberstamp the committee's recommendation — to the delight of the curriculum director or other change agent who very possibly had it planned that way months before.

Phase II (Programming) includes implementation of various new innovations, methodology, and textbooks chosen or designed to create the desired "product" — that product being children who think (and consequently behave) in a "prescribed" way. (Does the significance of "individualized" instruction now come into clear focus? The child is to be "diagnosed"; then, education to meet his "needs" can be "prescribed." Periodically he will be "evaluated," and can be "recycled" if necessary.)

Phase II also includes gaining school board approval and community acceptance of new programs.

PPBS may be implemented under some other name or acronym — "by some term that means *management by objectives*."[10]

To illustrate the ease with which change can be implemented, consider this bill,[11] passed by the Oregon Legislature in 1971, and now a part of Oregon Revised Statutes:

(1) The State Board of Education shall develop a state plan to insure the effective utilization of computerized automated data processing systems. . . .

(2) After July 1, 1971, districts utilizing or planning to utilize computerized automated data processing systems . . . shall submit to the State Board of Education a long-range plan for the utilization of the existing or proposed system.

(3) The State Board of Education shall review each plan submitted to determine whether it is consistent with the state plan developed pursuant to subsection (1) of this section and shall approve the plan or cause such revision in the

plan as is deemed necessary to make the plan consistent with the state plan. No district shall utilize a computerized automated data processing system that has not been approved by the state board.

(4) Nothing in this section is intended to require any district to purchase or rent equipment or purchase services for computerized automated data processing systems.

Probably nine out of ten Oregon parents do not even know this law is on the books and never heard of PPBS. (Many of them do know there is something drastically wrong with the education their children are receiving.)

This is not intended to imply that every computer in use, in Oregon or elsewhere, is a PPBS tool. Neither is it intended to imply that social engineers and "shapers" are not at work in those school districts where student records are not kept by computer. A computer, like other machines, can be used for good or bad purposes.

"The management of society as a whole demands the setting up of special machinery for the observation, control and ordering of each individual member of that society, if the whole is to function as the Planners desire."[12]

Combine the PPBS formula with various behavior modification techniques. Add a generous dose of the "New Education" theories and methodology. To that add computers. And next, through compulsory attendance laws, shove in forty-five million American children, and close the doors. The potential for capturing the minds and changing the beliefs of virtually an entire generation in a few short years staggers the imagination — and yet is undeniable.

Will you contribute your children as grist for their mills?

NOTES

1 Virginia McNeil "PPBS — The Conceptual Revolution," *The National Educator* (Fullerton, California), Vol. 4, No. 3, August, 1972, p. 20.

2 Deloris Feak, "A Look at the Full Scope of the New Education," mimeographed paper (an address prepared for a World History class at Saratoga Campus, West Valley College, Saratoga, California, June, 1972), p. 6 (hereafter cited as Deloris Feak, "New Education").

3 *Ibid.*, p. 5.

4 *Ibid.*, p. 6.

5 From C.M. Wa.d's Revivaltime Radio Sermon (No. 1022, July 8, 1973), "The Sin of Being Led Astray," in which he discusses the importance of "making ourselves inaccessible to the influence of others any farther than we choose.

6 Mary Thompson "PPBS," mimeographed paper (text of speech delivered to Santa Clara Republican Women Federated, January 18, 1972), p. 2.

7 *Ibid.*, pp. 2, 3.

8 *Ibid.* p. 3.

9 *Ibid.*, p. 4.

10 Mrs. Joseph P. Bean, "PPBS — Potential Perils Beyond Schooling," *Light:* Bi-Monthly Publication of the League of Men Voters of the United States, Inc., May-June, 1971, p. 1.

11 O.R.S. 326-081 (H.B. 1103).

12 "Proofs of a Conspiracy to Build a Total Managed Global Society," Number Seven, *Don Bell Reports: A Weekly Commentary,* No. 42, October 20, 1972, p. 1.

16

THE EQUALITY MYTH

Nowhere, except in God's value for each human soul on earth, does *equality* exist! It is a myth. *Equality* is not found in nature. . . .

. . . Col. Curtis B. Dall
F.D.R : My Exploited Father-in-Law

"Equality" in education is not only a myth; it is a physical impossibility. The number of dollars spent per child is not an accurate measuring stick as to the quality of education. Good textbooks in one school may cost less than poor textbooks in another. Children in a modest building with an intelligent, talented teacher (whose salary is relatively low) may be getting a far better education than other children in an elaborate building, with a better-paid, but less qualified teacher.

Having two teachers in identical adjoining rooms, each holders of identical degrees, using identical textbooks, and drawing identical salaries — would not guarantee equal education for the children involved. The human variable enters in; some are just better teachers than others.

Suppose two schools (one comprised of predominately Chinese-American children and another of white American children) were to offer identical buildings, identical textbooks, and teachers with identical degrees. Even though segregated, they would still be "equal" insofar as tangible facilities allow. Thus, neither segregation nor integration per se is the criterion for judging either the quality of "equality" of education.

The late Manning Johnson, a Negro, commented:

It is ·. . . implied that a Negro child is handicapped in his studies unless he is sitting beside a white child. What could be more nonsensical or ridiculous? It is a sad commentary on the ability of the Negro child to say that he cannot properly study

119

or that he will develop harmful complexes if he does not sit beside a white child. By what quirk of reasoning does one conclude that sitting beside a white child will help a Negro child
make the grade? Experience shows that a student's success is
determined by how much attention, time and effort he is
willing to put into his studies. [1]

It appears that neither the best education possible, nor the greatest
safety and welfare of children involved, is the primary concern of busing
proponents. Why should millions be spent for busing that could be spent
for improving school buildings, and for purchasing textbooks and
supplies for use in neighborhood schools?

What is the real goal of busing advocates? To improve education? Or
to break down ethnic, cultural, and religious differences? Is forced
busing one more tool to help bring social change in a predetermined
direction?

Should cultural differences be broken down? Is pluralism undesirable? Should Chinese, Indians, Mexicans, or Negroes be compelled to
merge into white culture? Why should their own unique customs and
cultures not be preserved through segregated schools for their children,
if voluntary segregation is their choice?

Have we lost our freedom of voluntary association?

It was the late Richard M. Weaver who said:

The right to self-segregate . . . is an indispensable ground of its
[a culture's] being . . . . our culture today is faced with very
serious threats in the form of rationalistic drives to prohibit, in
the name of equality, cultural segregation. The effect of this
would be to break up the natural cultural cohesion and to try to
replace it with artificial politically dictated integration.... This
crisis has been brought to our attention most spectacularly in
the attempt to "integrate" culturally distinct elements by court
action. It is, however, only the most publicized of the moves;
others are taking place in areas not in the spotlight, but all
originate in ignorance, if not in a suicidal determination to
write an end to the heritage of Western culture. [2]

"There was a time when the quality of performance determined the
right of a man or woman to rise or fall — according to his ability. But
today qualification and capacity and character are fast becoming

matters of secondary consideration." [3] The color of your skin or your sex may be more important. "A question is in order. How is it that, although only 12% of America's population is coloured, some 30 to 50% of America's athletes are black? Did the blacks simply get there because they were competent? More power to such." [4] Suppose the whites should demand pro-rated quotas in all professional sports. Ridiculous.

What about the Jews with less than three per cent of the population? "How did so many of them get to the top in *Who's Who*, the sciences, medicine, and the arts. . .? Should the Jews . . . be allowed to rise no higher than their quota. . .? Those who go off on a quota quirk had better return to sanity." [5]

Equality is graphically described by Erica Carle in *The Hate Factory* (a study on sociology in the schools). Here are some of her thoughts:

Freedom and enforced equality are irreconcilable opposites. Efforts to force economic and social equality only restrict freedom, thought, intelligence and productive capacity. Equality as a goal or dogma is a crippler and a killer.

Equality is the ceiling above which one dare not rise. . . .

Equality is the denial of nature, the rallying cry of the willfully blind. . . .

Equality is death of spirit, choice denied.

Equality is no mountains to climb, no barriers to leap, no dreams to make real.

Equality is a zombie, head lowered, never daring to look up, ahead, or to the side — marching at measured pace with all who deny individuality and self. [6]

If state officials can force you — against your will — to send your children to a particular school, how long will it be until they can force you — against your will — to live in a particular house in a particular part of town, or work at a particular job?

Forced integration is just as evil as forced segregation. The evil lies neither in integration nor in segregation, but in the use of force to achieve either.

NOTES

1 Manning Johnson, *Color, Communism and Common Sense* (New York: Alliance, Inc., 1958), p. 48.

2 Richard M. Weaver, *Visions of Order: The Cultural Crisis of Our Time,* paperback ed. (Baton Rouge: Louisiana State University Press, 1964; manufactured in the United States by Vail-Ballou Press, Inc., Binghamton, New York), p. 21.

3 L.E. Maxwell, "Perspective," *The Prairie Overcomer,* Vol. 45, No. 11, November, 1972, p. 504.

4 *Ibid.*

5 *Ibid.*

6 Erica Carle, *The Hate Factory* (Fullerton, California: Educator Publications, 1972); selected statements from pp. 62, 63.

17

SCHOOL PRAYERS AND RELIGIOUS DISCRIMINATION

Whose freedom is to be infringed and whose is to be respected?

> . . . Nicholas Wolterstorff
> *Religion and the Schools*

We have heard over and over again that the United States Supreme Court has not ruled against voluntary prayer in public schools. There is probably more misunderstanding as to whether or not children can voluntarily pray in the public schools, than any other educational issue. Of course, not even a Supreme Court Justice can prevent a child from praying silently. But what about audible, voluntary, individual or group prayer? What about voluntary prayer before lunch — in the presence of some who may object?

Technically any prayer is "prescribed" either by the one doing the praying or previously by another. Since no state official or teacher can "prescribe" any particular prayer — not even the Lord's Prayer — who can? What prayers can be said? Where in the building can a prayer be said? Who will decide?

The First Amendment to the Constitution provides that:

"Congress shall make no law respecting an establishment of religion, or prohibiting the free exercise thereof."

Prayer, unquestionably, is an exercise of religion.

In various cases in which the High Court has ruled against prayer and Bible reading in public schools (including cases where children of dissenting parents were permitted to leave the room), the Establishment of Religion clause was deemed to have been violated, because the exercises were the result of state or school board laws, rulings, or directives.

What about a case where a state has passed a law requiring prayer or

Bible reading or both? Where a state or local board has adopted a policy or issued a directive requiring the daily reading of the Bible or prayer (excusing those unwilling to participate)? Conceivably, such cases could be construed as an establishment of religion.

But, what about cases where no state or local action required prayer? Cases where prayer was strictly voluntary?

Take the Netcong, New Jersey, case.[1] Students who wished to do so were permitted to go to the gymnasium at 7:55 A.M. to participate in reading prayers or remarks from the Congressional Record. Students who did not wish to participate could go directly to their homerooms, or could delay their arrival at school until the conclusion of the prayer exercise.

The State Commissioner of Education requested an opinion from the State Attorney General as to the constitutionality of the practice. The State Attorney General's opinion was that the practice did violate the Constitution.

Following a suit brought by the State Board against the Netcong Board, a Superior Court judge ordered the school to immediately cease the practice. He held that the program violated the Establishment Clause of the Constitution, and he rejected the argument that the local board was defending the free exercise of religion.

The lower court ruling was affirmed by the Supreme Court of New Jersey in a *per curiam* opinion on November 9, 1970.

On April 5, 1971, the United States Supreme Court denied the petition for writ of *certiorari* without an opinion. This means the Supreme Court refused to hear the case. This left standing the opinion of the New Jersey Supreme Court of November 9, 1970, which forbid voluntary reading of prayers.

In another case (*Stein* v. *Oshinsky*)[2] school officials (defendants) had prevented kindergarten children from voluntarily saying these two prayers:

God is great	Thank you for the world so sweet
God is good	Thank you for the food we eat
And we thank Him	Thank you for the birds that sing
For our food.	Thank you God for everything.

The District Court prohibited the defendants from interfering with the prayers.

The case was appealed. The Court of Appeals "pointed out that the State of New York and its political subdivisions could refuse to permit prayers in schools unless the United States Constitution . . . compelled a different result." [3]

In the *Netcong* case, children were voluntarily assembling for the purpose of reading a prayer or other remarks from the Congressional Record.

In the *Stein* v. *Oshinsky* case, children already assembled were forbidden to voluntarily participate in prayer.

By refusing to review such cases, the United States Supreme Court acted. They acted against voluntary prayer by letting lower court rulings stand which forbid voluntary prayer.

To forbid children to pray voluntarily is most assuredly an infringement upon the free exercise of the religion of children who wish to do so.

If Congress shall make no law "prohibiting the free exercise" of religion, should the Supreme Court, through action or inaction, forbid the free exercise thereof?

Freedom is the right to participate or refrain from participating. Both Christians and non-Christians, including secular humanists, had these rights when voluntary prayers were permitted. But when that right is denied, then the rights of Christians are trampled upon. Such action clearly favors the religion of nontheistic Humanism over theistic religion.

Some will contend that when a non-participating child has to leave the classroom that child may suffer embarrassment or emotional distress, and that such a situation constitutes a form of compulsion or social duress.

For decades children whose parents, for religious reasons, objected to dancing in public schools were subjected to being classified as "different." Who expressed any concern for their "embarrassment"? Did anyone suggest the whole class stop dancing because it was against the religion of a few?

Restrictions upon the Constitutional "free exercise" of religion, resulting from Supreme Court rulings in recent years, raise serious questions as to the Constitutionality of state compulsory education laws.

Public schools are now a function of government. If it is Constitutionally "wrong" to permit voluntary prayers in the public school, why isn't it "wrong" to offer prayer in Congress? To have "In God We Trust" on our coins? The answer is clear. One who is intellectually honest, has but to consider, with an open mind, the various documental treasures of our history to realize that eliminating God from various functions of government was never the intent of the founding fathers. Their intent was to insure and protect the right to the free exercise of religion, while avoiding the establishment of a state church.

Teaching *About* Religion

Some try to quiet the issue by reminding us that public schools can teach about religion. This possibility may salve the naive, but serious questions are likely to surface in the minds of the deeper-thinking.

How many teachers can teach objectively (without prejudice) about a religion contradictory to their own? How many can teach objectively (without favoritism) about their own religion? How many Catholic parents would want a Baptist to instruct their children in this area? How many Mormons would permit a Christian Scientist to teach their children about religion? How many Unitarians would agree to let an evangelical teach their children about religion?

Will children be brought to believe that all religions are equally valid? Will Christianity be studied as modernism or as fundamentalism? Will the Bible be presented as Divinely inspired? Will Jesus be considered as only a human person or as the Divine Son of God?

Where does the greater danger for indoctrination lie — in teaching children about religion, or in permitting children to voluntarily pray to God, the Creator of all mankind, and read a verse of Scripture together without comment?

Regardless of what the Supreme Court did or did not rule, it has succeeded in muddying the waters and creating enough confusion and misunderstanding that the name of God has been virtually eliminated from our public school system, except where sometimes used in a profane manner in contemporary trash guised as "literature." By what line of reasoning can a child who cannot be required to repeat the name of God honorably in a simple prayer be required to read "literature" which uses that Holy Name profanely?

A Solution

A solution which would very quickly settle the prayer issue is a simple amendment to the United States Constitution which provides that:

The right of persons lawfully assembled, in any public building which is supported in whole or in part through the expenditure of public funds, to participate in voluntary prayer shall not be infringed.

With 402 voting, a voluntary prayer amendment fell a mere twenty-eight votes short of the two-thirds majority needed to pass the House of Representatives in 1971.

Nine bills that would have permitted prayer in public schools were introduced in Congress in January 1973. A voluntary prayer amendment can succeed when enough people become sufficiently concerned to be heard by their elected representatives and senators, over the voices of highly organized liberal or misled church factions and humanist and atheist activists.

Neutrality or Humanism?

Justice Tom C. Clark, who wrote the majority opinion in the Schempp case in 1963, quoted Judge Alphonzo Taft who, nearly 100 years ago, said, "The government is neutral and while protecting all, it prefers none, and disparages none."

A court action which forbids little children from saying "Thank you God for everything" (or any other prayer on a strictly voluntary basis) in the public school house, does indeed "disparage some."

Cardinal Patrick O'Boyle spoke out articulately in Washington, D.C., in 1971, calling "public school neutrality" to religion a myth. He asserted:

I believe experience shows and will increasingly show that public schools inevitably are more favorable to one religion or another. It may be argued that public schools need not favor any particular religion, or any religion at all, because they can proceed on strictly humanistic, pragmatic, and secular conceptions.

But this is precisely the point. To proceed in this way is itself to establish a religion — secular humanism — and to favor this religion over all others. [4]

If we must have a state church via the public school system, who voted for Secular Humanism?

The Booher Story

An Oregon couple, Mr. and Mrs. Charles Booher, are devout Christians who wanted their young daughter's education to be "based on the teaching of facts and the principles of the Scriptures." [5]   They objected to the content of some public school textbooks, to sensitivity training, and to the theory of evolution.

The Boohers prefer to live quietly and peaceably. Their neat, secluded home sits on an attractively landscaped clearing among stately firs. The sign on a small modern building nearby reads:

BEAR CREEK

Private

SCHOOL

Nine-year-old Melody Ann, with her parents as teachers, began work by correspondence course in September, 1970. At the time, her fifteen-year-old sister was studying by correspondence course, as the four older Booher children had done after finishing public elementary school. That Fall, Melody Ann and her sister were the only students attending Bear Creek Private School.

In December, 1970, the county school superintendent filed a complaint against the Boohers. On January 25, 1971, Mr. and Mrs. Booher, who radiate courage, independence, and faith in God, had their day in court.

Melody Ann, while in the third grade in public school the previous school year, had scored 4.5 (fourth grade, fifth month). In December, after a few months in her parents' private school, she scored an average of 7.1 (seventh grade, first month).

Nevertheless, the Boohers were convicted and fined.

Undaunted and determined, they did not send Melody Ann back to the public school. They appealed.

The following May, when the case came up again, they were acquitted. Melody Ann, present in the courtroom when the verdict was read, handed her sister a quickly written note. It simply said:

"What God hath wrought."

Financial Penalties

There are other ways to discriminate against a person besides making him ride in the back of the bus. One of the most effective ways this can be done is to penalize him financially for his beliefs.

It cost the Boohers hundred of dollars in legal fees to defend their constitutional rights and to prove their innocence.

> It is often said that the rights of those who cannot in good conscience send their children to the public school are adequately protected by allowing them to establish their own schools. And in our country those who, for whatever reason, dislike the public school do have the long-established right, the *legal* right, to establish their own schools. . . . [But] common sense, as well as various of the Court's opinions, tells us that a legal arrangement whereby a financial penalty is attached to the exercise of someone's religion can constitute an infringement on the free exercise of that religion — that is, can constitute coercive discrimination against that religion. [6]

Why should parents who wish to provide a better education for their children than the public schools offer, be harassed or financially penalized?

Not all parents are financially able to defend their Constitutional rights in court as the Boohers did. Consequently, they bow their knee to Caesar and continue sending their children to Caesar's church-school.

George Charles Roche III explained the matter this way:

> Across this nation, those parents who would exercise responsible choice in the education of their children are penalized for their responsible behavior. Parents who would place their children in a private school more responsive to their values and attitudes are advised by the tax collector, "First support the State's educational philosophy; then, if you have any surplus resources, you may pursue *your* educational philosophy." [7]

Such action is undeniably in violation of the Constitutional rights of parents who prefer private schools. It is a form of discrimination. For "a financial burden is placed on those with certain conscientious convictions that is not placed on those lacking these convictions." [8]

Among our "unalienable rights" endowed by our Creator are "life, liberty, and the pursuit of happiness." Do state laws or United States Supreme Court rulings which restrict a man's liberty in the choice of his children's education not indeed interfere with that man's pursuit of happiness?

In order for parents and children to enjoy the freedom of religion that writers of the Constitution intended, there must be an "unabridged right of each parent to educate his child in full accord with his own religious convictions." [9] And that must be without harassment or financial penalty.

NOTES

1 See "Recent Developments in the Area of Religious Activities in Public Schools and Other Public Places," LC 111, 71-269A, 467/98 (R), Herbert A. Danner, February 28, 1969; Revised and updated by David H. Baris, Legislative Attorney, American Law Division, September 15, 1971, with Addendum November 9, 1971; Congressional Research Service, Library of Congress, pp. CRS-19, 20, 21.

2 *Ibid.,* pp. CRS-8, 9.

3 *Ibid.,* p. CRS-9.

4 "Cardinal Says Public Schools Promote 'Secular Humanism' As Official Religion," *The Pentecostal Evangel,* December 12, 1971, p. 27.

5 "Private School Controversy, 'Anything Can Happen Now' Says Boohers," *Roseburg* (Ore.) *News-Review,* June 7, 1971.

6 Nicholas Wolterstorff, *Religion and the Schools,* A Reformed Journal Monograph (Grand Rapids, Michigan: William B. Eerdmans Publishing Company, 1965, 1966), pp. 41, 42; (first appeared in slightly different form in *Reformed Journal*); (hereafter cited Wolterstorff, *Religion and the Schools*).

7 George Charles Roche III, *Education in America* (Irvington-on-Hudson, New York: The Foundation for Economic Education, Inc., 1969; ©1969 by George Charles Roche III), p. 152.

8 Wolterstorff, *Religion and the Schools,* p. 36.

9 *Ibid.,* p. 24.

18

A STATE CHURCH IN DISGUISE

Belief in man or man's mind as the highest good (humanism) is, from all appearances, the state or national religion today. And the tax-supported public school system is by far the most powerful and all pervasive "state church" through which that religion is being propagated.

                                                  . . . Ruth Denison
                                            former high school teacher

In order to grasp the significance of various aspects of the New Education, it is important we have an understanding of the religion of Secular Humanism.

Humanism negates the Genesis account of creation and believes that man is a product of the processes of evolution. Humanism refuses to acknowledge the existence of an Omnipotent, Supernatural God.

Humanism repudiates the Divinity of Jesus. The Bible is not accepted as Divinely inspired. The Humanist acknowledges no such thing as "sin" in the Biblical sense, and consequently admits no need of a Savior. Acceptance of Biblical Absolutes as ultimate authority in matters of morality is rejected.

The executive director of the American Humanist Association, Keith Beggs, in 1973 was quoted in a Religious News Service release as stating:

Humanists are concerned with breaking loose from all angles and aspects of traditional morality, from the old concepts of what is moral behavior. Humanistic beliefs on morality, when explicitly expressed, come very close to what's called the "new morality," which is a relativistic approach. [1]

Humanism dismisses the idea of conscious life after death, rejecting belief in a literal heaven and hell as described in Scripture.

Humanism "considers the complete realization of human personality

131

to be the end of man's life and seeks its development . . . in the here and now," according to Humanist Manifesto I, issued in 1933.

Humanists are still striving "for the good life, here and now." [2] Humanist Manifesto II, issued in 1973, states: "The ultimate goal should be the fulfillment of the potential for growth in each human personality — not for the favored few, but for all of humankind. Only a shared world and global measures will suffice." [3]

How is this to be accomplished? "No deity will save us; we must save ourselves," [4] they declare. "Traditional religions" are seen as "obstacles to human progress." [5] The "positive principles" they affirm "are a design for a secular society on a planetary scale." [6] Secular means without God. Planetary means world-wide.

Humanists endorse a "world community" and believe that "the best option is to *transcend the limits of national sovereignty*. . . . Thus we look to the development of a system of world law and a world order based upon transnational federal government." [7]

Charles Francis Potter (one of the signers of Humanist Manifesto I) defined Humanism as *"faith in the supreme value and self-perfectibility of human personality* [8] . . . . Human personality is . . . perfectible by no other agency than the self." [9]

In public education today increasing stress is being placed upon the importance of the child having a *positive self-concept*. This simply means the child sees a good picture of himself, or thinks favorably of himself. Increasingly noticeable in educational materials for teachers are such terms as: self-concept, self-esteem, self-awareness, self-acceptance, self-fulfillment, self-realization, self-actualization.

Self. Self. Self.

Is there anything wrong with so much concern about the child's "self"?

A noted psychologist was asked, "How do you explain to parents that the 'self-acceptance' doctrine could be harmful?" Her terse reply was, "Where does self-acceptance end and self-aggrandizement begin?"

Where does self-esteem end and arrogance begin? How do the Christian attributes of meekness and humility fit into the pattern? If we completely accept ourselves as we are — in sin — will we feel our need to come to Christ for forgiveness?

How much concern with "self" is compatible with Christianity? The

Bible offers this directive: ". . . but in lowliness of mind let each esteem other better than themselves." (Phil. 2:3b).

Did Christ say, "Whosoever will come after me," — let him first accept himself? No! Rather, ". . . let him deny himself, and take up his cross, and follow me." [10]

No place in Scripture are parents admonished:

Thou shalt give thy child a positive self-concept.

Thou shalt build his self-esteem.

Thou shalt help him achieve self-acceptance.

This does not mean Christian parents are to reject, neglect, belittle or discourage their children. Quite the contrary. Through example, teaching, and precept, parents are to bring their children up "in the nurture and admonition of the Lord." [11] Such children can be secure in the knowledge that their parents love and care for them — not only for their material and physical needs — but for their eternal welfare, as well. "Perfect love casteth out fear." [12] There is no room for inferiority complex here.

The Apostle Paul, one of the most learned men of his day, (having studied under Gamaliel), declared, "What things were gain to me, those I counted loss . . . . that I may win Christ." [13] He also asserted he had "no confidence in the flesh," [14] but that he could "do all things through Christ" [15] — The Source of his strength.

The Humanist places his faith in man's intellect and reason and in "scientific method." The Christian places his faith in the Creator of man Who endowed man with intellect and reason, including the mental capacity to understand and employ "scientific method."

The Christian seeks to know God. The existentialist-humanist says, "Know thyself."

> The idea [of knowing oneself] sounds good but the fact remains that none of us has the capacity to see ourselves as we really are by searching down inside ourselves. . . . A great deal of self-searching outside of Jesus Christ breeds nothing but disillusionment and despair. . . . The only one who really knows us is the God who made us and if we are to know ourselves, we must see ourselves as God sees us. [16]

What kind of answers are children getting or finding to the "Who am I?" question in public schools?

Both optimistic humanism and the existentialist breed of humanism encourage self-awareness. This might help explain the use of
"self-understanding," "self-awareness," sensory awareness, group
therapy, role-playing, and other potentially dangerous sensitivity training techniques in some classrooms. Self-awareness exercises begin in the
first grade in some schools.

Self-awareness and body-awareness are introvertive. "Any system that
leaves you occupied with yourself is wrong, however learned it may be."[17]

The current infatuation with giving children a "positive self-concept"
should offer a clue to the rash of "humane" innovations such as
non-grading, non-competition, and no-failure schools now being
promoted.

Humanistic psychology (also called Third Force psychology, as differentiated from psychoanalysis and behaviorism) encourages *self-
actualization,* or the attainment of your greatest potential. (Christians
also believe man should strive to reach his utmost potential but, for a
different reason, and by a different means than the Humanist.)

What's going to happen to the "self-actualizing," non-competing
children when they get out into the real dog-eat-dog world where they
won't be pampered and "positively reinforced" for every insipid effort
they make? Where progressing-at-their-own-rate may be just a little too
slow? Where they have to compete in the market place? What's going to
happen to overblown self-concepts then? How can they cope with failures
in life — which come to all of us in varying degrees — if they have been
protected from simple embarrassments and small psychic wounds such
as getting a "D" on a report card?

Or do the "humane" educators and their humanistic psychologist
mentors figure, with a herd of this calibre of young people, a New Age of
Socialistic Humanism will rush in where all will "cooperate" rather than
"compete"? Where the New Generation can live and work and play with
the blissful contentment of docile sheep, a "shared life in a shared
world," performing their tasks willingly, as "humane" facilitators
dangle "positive reinforcement" rewards?

Are American children being conditioned to trade their precious
birthright of freedom under God for a mess of humanist pottage?

And there is in the idea of "self-actualization" apart from God a
pitfall to which the young, particularly, are susceptible. Professor

Duncan Williams (while admitting he basically has no quarrel with "views which uphold the substitution of individual . . . standards for the old-fashioned, legalistic and external ones"[18]), describes the danger this way:

> [Between] the old morality and the new self-fulfillment (or "self-actualization"), there exists a chasm into which, while attempting to cross, the majority falls. This chasm is self-indulgence, a descent to mere animal gratification, which presents the greatest danger to the immature who, vaguely aware of the demise of the old sanctions, delight in the permissiveness which increasingly pervades our society. [19]

Williams believes "self-fulfillment" is an adult concept which demands a measure of restraint and self-control. [20]

And there is yet another trap into which the self-actualized may step. It snared the learned Saul of Tarsus who had reached a pinnacle of self-actualization. His talents and energies, in spite of his sincerity, were spent destructively as he persecuted Christians. It was only after he was struck blind on the road to Damascus and became *Christ*-conscious and forfeited his own "positive" *self*-concept, that his life became a power for good.

Probably one of history's most self-actualized men was Adolf Hitler. Where did his "positive self-concept" take the world?

The Biblical, Christian position is that the greatest possible fulfillment of a man's life is attained only as his life and especially *self* is placed at the disposal of Another whose wisdom surpasses his own. Then his talents and efforts, his intelligence and reason can be used under Divine Guidance for good.

True, man apart from God may achieve great things, may reach great heights. And some do. This is so because, even though he is alienated from God, man is still a specially-endowed creature. He is still the beneficiary of God's blessings. He enjoys the use of his God-given faculties even though he denies or ignores the Creator of those faculties. But regardless of how much a man accomplishes in himself, through his own intelligence, he could accomplish even more (for good) were his life totally committed to Christ. There are several reasons this is true.

Disentangled from detrimental physical habits (such as liquor, cigarettes, and drugs) and set free from mental aggravations (such as worry, greed, resentment, indecision, oversensitivity, self-centeredness, jealousy, guilt and fear), the genuine Christian man can know what it means to be truly free. With his mind not entangled in the web of materialist-relativist thought-forms, he is free to think, intelligently and independently. His thinking enjoys a dimension materialist-relativist thinking lacks; he has a longer range and a broader view.

The Christian is far less likely than the non-Christian to fall into the chasm of self-indulgence and animal gratification mentioned by Williams.

When the Christian is confronted with seemingly insurmountable difficulties, he has more than his own limited intelligence, more than his own reason, more than modern science offers, from which to draw. With the power of an Omnipotent God moving, enlightening, and strengthening him, he becomes the instrument through which far more can be accomplished than he could ever hope to achieve by his own strength and knowledge alone. This becomes possible when he places himself — his very *self* — at God's disposal. He can walk with quiet confidence because he knows with certainty that he is on the right road. *He knows, not only who he is, but where he has been and where he is going.*

In contrast modern humanists with their gospel of self-actualization are reminiscent of Adam and Eve:

Adam and Eve let themselves be so hoodwinked as to seek their freedom in independence of God. They are the prototypes of modern man. . . . They thought by doing so to become like God, absolutely free, independent selves grounded in themselves. . . .

. . . [Modern man] wants to be independent of God as he ought to be independent of the world. But by cutting himself loose from God in order to become free, . . . he loses that Archimedean fulcrum outside the world by which he really could move the world. By cutting himself loose from God, man precipitates himself into the world and becomes its prisoner. Man liberated from God becomes the slave of the world. [21]

By turning loose of God, man indeed forfeits his greatest opportunity for "growth" and "becoming" — to use humanistic terms. By turning loose of God, he settles at best for second best. And he may fall far short, even of that. For, as a prisoner of the world, he may find himself engulfed in a quagmire of self-centeredness and greed, trapped in a marshland of alcoholism, lost in a jungle of loose, immoral living, or simply contentedly sidetracked in a suburban cul-de-sac of *self*-ish living.

Rushdoony tells us, "The intellectual stance now is a radical cynicism and relativism . . . but every critique is in terms of a criterion, and the criterion of the intellectuals is a deep faith in the reason of autonomous intellectual man." [22] Autonomous man is a man who has ripped asunder his association with God.

The existentialist says because man has autonomous freedom, he has awesome responsibility. If God is dead, then man is Lord; and there is no longer an Absolute Standard by which to test one's beliefs or to measure one's conduct and choices. Hence the awesome responsibility of choosing. So, Man the Ultimate must stand responsible for his choices.

It is important to understand this existentialist vein of humanistic thinking because of emphasis in public education in recent years on the "Fourth R: Responsibility." Students must be responsible for the choices they make. Responsible to God? No. Responsible to the Great God Society.

Now, Christians believe in responsibility, too. They recognize their responsibility to God for their choices and behavior. It is the knowledge that we are ultimately responsible to God that helps us behave as we ought. When man is truly responsible to God and honors His Standard, all else falls into place.

What many humanists perhaps do not realize, or would be reluctant to admit, is that many of their "responsible" actions result from standards substantially seasoned with the salt of Christian presuppositions, which have influenced and helped to preserve our whole Western civilization for generations. In other words, while they renounce or shun Christianity, much of their own "responsible" conduct stems from the influence of the very Christianity they renounce.

As we have already noted, Humanism *"might be defined as man's effort to solve his problems and shape his society apart from God."* [23] Is that not precisely what public schools all across this land are attempting to teach children to do?

To instill in children a method of social or personal problem-solving which omits the vertical dimension — as if God did not exist or count —

is to promote a secular, humanistic approach. The upward look gives problems a whole new dimension, and offers different solutions than a strictly humanistic approach.

To teach children to make "value judgments" (which include decisions on moral issues) without consideration of Divine Laws is to direct them down a humanist path.

To teach the theory of evolution, while ignoring or denying the Genesis account of Creation is undeniably to favor the religion of Humanism over Christianity.

To promote the acceptance of a world government over national sovereignty is to promote a humanist concept.

Requiring children to read existentialist literature subjectively (while failing to tell them they need not remain in alienation, that life need not be meaningless, that there is a Solution to man's dilemma, that there is a Light that can penetrate the dense gray fog of relativism, that there is a Way out of the dark chasm), is to favor the existentialist vein of Humanism over Christianty. It is the knowledge that God is really there, that He made us in His Own image and that He cares for each of us as individuals — that gives life meaning.

To promote self-actualization in a strictly secular manner is to promote a concept of humanistic psychology.

To teach children "to cope" with life and death as if there were nothing beyond death is to favor Humanism over Christianity.

To require children to take part in sensitivity training (self-awareness exercises, group therapy, etc.) is to subject them to techniques of humanistic psychology.

To undermine the Christian concepts of Certainty and Absolute Truth in favor of "probabilism" and relativism (tentativeness) is clearly to favor the religion of Humanism over Christianity.

To imbed in children's minds a pattern of thinking which promotes agnosticism, in the guise of teaching children "to think," is a gross deception. Agnosticism is a fellow traveler of Humanism.

To teach children "verification" through "inquiry" as the *sole* test of truth or fact is to teach a humanistic premise; this teaching relegates all discourse about God to the "opinion" scrap heap. "Aiming to teach the pupils no doctrine, they are yet taught [implicitly if not explicitly] that the doctrines of Christianity are not true. By the 'scientific method' the pupils are taught to share in a 'common faith.' " [24]

According to Dewey then, the teachers must present to the pupils . . . a philosophy of reality which absolutely excludes Christianity. This philosophy of reality is said to be involved in the adoption of the modern scientific methodology. For this scientific method involves the idea of ultimate change. And as such it must exclude the notion of the God of Christianity who is forever the same. [25]

In the final analysis, is there such a thing as religious neutrality in education? All education must have a reason for its existence, an underlying philosophy, and presuppositions and beliefs regarding the nature of the universe, the nature of man and the purpose of learning. There is no escaping this. These philosophies and beliefs will inevitably be reflected in the textbooks, films, and methodologies.

"The Christian principle presupposes God who speaks authoritatively through the Bible, giving man basic principles for the interpretation of the whole of life. The non-Christian principle presupposes man who speaks authoritatively of himself. . . ." [26] One is Christianity; the other is Humanism. And they are not compatible. Which beliefs are being reflected and promoted in classrooms?

Caesar's Church

More than forty years ago Charles Francis Potter wrote in his book, *Humanism, A New Religion:*

Education is thus a most powerful ally of Humanism, and every American public school is a school of Humanism. What can the theistic Sunday-schools, meeting for an hour once a week, and teaching only a fraction of the children, do to stem the tide of a five-day program of humanistic teaching? [27]

Do we have a state church — an establishment of religion via the public school system?

A *religion* is a set of beliefs held by a group of people. It need not be a set of beliefs about God. (Taoism, Buddhism, and Secular Humanism, for example, have been recognized in a United States Supreme Court decision, as religions that do not teach a belief in God.) [28]

A *church* is an institution through which religious beliefs are propagated.

An *establishment of religion* or a *state church* is one which is financially supported by the state or one at which the state requires attendance.

Our founding fathers took special care to avoid the tyranny of a state church. Have we proceeded in the twentieth century to permit the very despotism they sought to avoid?

Mr. Justice Hugo Black, in a dissenting opinion in *Board of Education Central School* v. *James E. Allen* (a case involving loaning of secular textbooks to parochial schools) stated:

> The *Everson* and *McCollum* cases plainly interpret the First and Fourteenth Amendments as protecting the taxpayers of a State from being compelled to pay taxes to their government to support the agencies of private religious organizations the taxpayers oppose. [29]

Taxpayers are to be protected from being compelled to pay taxes to support the agencies of private religious organizations they oppose. Why then should Christian taxpayers be required to pay taxes to support a public religious organization (alias public education) whose teachings they oppose?

Mr. Justice Black in the same dissenting opinion (quoting from a previous case), stated:

> No tax in any amount, large or small, can be levied to support any religious activities or institutions, whatever they may be called, or whatever form they may adopt to teach or practice religion. [30]

Were this to be consistently applied, tax funding of virtually all public schools in this nation would be cut immediately.

And Mr. Justice Black further stated:

> To authorize a State to tax its residents for such church purposes [loaning secular textbooks to a parochial school] is to put the State squarely in the religious activities of certain religious groups that happen to be strong enough politically to write their own religious preferences and prejudices into the laws. This links state and churches together in controlling the lives and destinies of our citizenship. . . . [31]

Does our public school system not indeed fall squarely into the category described by Justice Black? Is the state not now squarely in the business of furthering and promoting the religion of Secular Humanism?

When attendance and financing through taxation are compulsory, do we not indeed have all the criteria of an establishment of religion — a state church of Secular Humanism?

Dr. John F. Blanchard, Jr., (former executive director, National Association of Christian Schools), states it this way:

Secular education has its faith and its values, and these have a decidedly religious impact. This religion, called secular humanism with its commitment to these specific values is being proclaimed in tax-supported classrooms. This is an establishment of religion in its deepest sense. . . . The use of tax money to support this teaching significantly assails the constitutional rights of Bible-believing citizens. [32]

NOTES

1 "P.E. News Digest," *The Pentecostal Evangel,* No. 3089, July 22, 1973, p. 23.

2 *Humanist Manifesto II,* (San Francisco, California: American Humanist Association), n.d. [issued in 1973].

3 *Ibid.*

4 *Ibid.*

5 *Ibid.*

ɔ *Ibid.*

7 *Ibid.*

8 Charles Francis Potter, *Humanism, A New Religion* (New York: Simon and Schuster, MCMXXX, ©1930 by Charles Francis Potter; printed U.S.A. by Vail-Ballou Press, Binghamton, N.Y.), p. 14 (hereafter cited as Potter, *Humanism, A New Religion*).

9 *Ibid.,* p. 41.

10 Mark 8:34b.

11 Eph. 6:4b.

12 I John 4:18b.

13 See Phil. 3:7,8.

14 Phil. 3:3b.

15 Phil. 4:13b.

16 Jessie Rice Sandberg, "Somebody Important," *Sword of the Lord,* September 13, 1974.

17 E. Stanley Jones, *The Way to Power and Poise* (New York, Nashville:

Abingdon-Cokesbury Press; © MCMXLIX by Pierce & Smith), p. 14.

18 Duncan Williams, *Trousered Apes* (New Rochelle, New York: Arlington House, 1972; Churchill Press Limited, England, 1971), p. 35, American Edition.

19 *Ibid.*, p. 36.

20 *Ibid.*, p. 35.

21 Emil Brunner, *Christianity and Civilisation*, Vol. I (New York: Charles Scribner's Sons, 1948), pp. 132, 133.

22 Rousas John Rushdoony, *Chalcedon Report No. 88*, December, 1972, p. 3.

23 H. Edward Rowe, *Humanism*, supplement to *Christian Economics*, n.d.

24 Cornelius Van Til, *The Dilemma of Education*, second ed. (Presbyterian and Reformed Publishing Co., 1956; first ed., published by National Union of Christian Schools), p. 6.

25 *Ibid.*, p. 7.

26 *Ibid.*, p. 40.

27 Potter, *Humanism, A New Religion*, p. 128.

28 Torcaso case, 1961.

29 Supreme Court of the United States, No. 660, October Term, 1967, opinion June 10, 1968.

30 *Ibid.*

31 *Ibid.*

32 John F. Blanchard, Jr., *Myths of Public Education*, brochure (Wheaton, Ill.: National Association of Christian Schools; ©1972 by Good News Broadcasting Association, Inc.).

19

A LOOK AT ALTERNATIVES

There can be no freedom in any sphere where one is denied alternative.

. . . George W. Seevers
history teacher

It must be acknowledged there are parents who will go "to court in defense of their little darlings' right to attend classes while looking . . . like chimpanzees. Too bad they are not equally militant in demanding that their children at least learn to read and write while attending."[1]

There are parents who actually prefer permissiveness, "creativity," "spontaneity," and "social-adjustment," for their children, to disciplined learning.

There are those who not only want their children taught no moral absolutes, they want them taught there are no moral absolutes.

There are parents who prefer, for their children, affective (emotional) learning experiences, including sensitivity training in various forms, to intellectual exercises, such as memorization of the multiplication tables.

There are parents who want their children to read Eldridge Cleaver's *Soul on Ice,* Richard Wright's *Black Boy,* James Baldwin's *Another Country,* and J.D. Salinger's *The Catcher in the Rye.*

There are multitudes of other parents who are sick of stupid look-say readers, biased social studies, shoddy and offensive literature, time-wasting films, and sensitivity training.

They detest having to send their children into a social environment where they must rub shoulders with pot-smoking, filthy-mouthed, V.D.-infected degenerates.

There are parents who do not want their children taught relativism unless the existence of Permanent and Absolute Truth is also acknowledged. They do not want their children taught the doctrine of "probability" as though Certainty were not possible.

Some parents would prefer schools where children are taught to read and write fluently, and to spell correctly.

They would welcome schools where factual history and geography are taught as such, and not diluted or lost in homogenized "social studies" or replaced by "relevant" social problem-solving.

They would like their children to learn the unvarnished truth about the United Nations — who instigated it, who controls it, where it will take us, and what it has and has not accomplished.

They would like their children to study both predominate views of the origin of earth and man, objectively.

They would welcome schools where genuine academic learning, teacher-directed learning, would be given priority over "adjustment" and "social interaction." They would prefer schools where teachers are expected to teach, and not assume the role of fellow-learner, quack-psychologist, change agent, "healer," or social leveler.

Can the Public Schools Be Salvaged?

If by salvaged we mean restored to their original, proper function of academic learning, the answer is yes. Even at this late hour, if certain groups of persons would do what they are duty bound to do — but in most cases are not doing — public schools could be restored to a modicum of common sense.

Let's consider some of the ways these groups can aid in the restoration of public education to its rightful purpose.

(1) Public schools could be salvaged if *all* school board members would recognize and assume their rightful obligations to the constituents of their districts.

They are in a position to call a halt to the present push to turn public schools into psyc..-social clinics. Removing psychologists from educational payrolls would be an immediate step in the right direction.

School boards should refuse to permit teachers to attend in-service training sessions at district expense, when such sessions include sensitivity training in any form. And, they should realize that such workshops are not likely to be labelled "sensitivity training." They should issue and enforce directives that no teacher shall use sensitivity training techniques of any kind in the classroom.

They should refuse to approve programs incorporating behavior modification techniques, such as operant conditioning.

No child should be required to participate in any pilot or experimental program to which his parents object.

Plans of the PPBSers could be shattered if school board members would refuse to approve textbooks and methodology aimed at changing children's attitudes, beliefs, and values; they should forbid testing and record-keeping in these areas. They should also provide that all student cumulative files be available for parental inspection.

School board members have an obligation to see that the purpose of elementary education is accomplished. That purpose is to equip each child with the tools of reading, writing, and arithmetic — the tools with which he may later become educated. Unless this is the purpose, and unless this purpose can be realized, continued existence of public schools is not justifiable.

School board members are duty bound to take action that forbids lopsided humanistic presentations of the origin of the earth and of man. Such action should provide that both predominate views (Genesis and the evolutionary religion) are taught objectively on an equal time basis — or that neither is taught.

School board members should issue and enforce directives forbidding teachers to favor or promote the religion of Secular Humanism in any form, either explicitly or implicitly. In order to accomplish this, school board members themselves would need a thorough understanding of both Christianity and Humanism. They also need to exercise enough moral stamina to be more than rubber stamps for smooth-talking administrators.

Any school board member who considers himself "unqualified" to judge textbook content (and must leave those decisions to teacher committees or to a highly paid curriculum administrator), is "unqualified" to occupy a seat on the school board. What is his reason for being there? If he is "too busy" to examine textbooks, he is "too busy" to serve on a school board.

(2) Public schools could be salvaged if all evangelical, Bible-believing ministers would inform themselves and then assume their rightful obligation to protect children in their own congregations.

Imagine the impact of consecrated ministers, (even occasionally), accompanying entire, informed congregations to school board meetings.

Imagine the possible results, were these ministers to speak authoritative-ly, on behalf of their people, requesting removal of objectionable textbooks, films, or methodology from the classrooms on the grounds of violation of their religious beliefs. Would school boards dare not listen?

(3) Public schools could be salvaged if Christian school teachers, (after first gaining a thorough understanding of humanistic philosophies as intertwined in curriculum and methodology in their own districts), would then organize and resist en masse. It is not enough that they individually handle objectionable materials in an inoffensive manner, insofar as possible. They are duty bound as Christians to expose and oppose the infiltration of Secular Humanism in the public schools.

Through past decades, many dedicated teachers have worked nobly to teach young children basic skills; they have instilled, through example and precept, character-building thoughts. They have taught children the importance of good citizenship. Thank God for those teachers, and for those teachers today who have not succumbed to the humanistic philosophy of education. Thank God for those who are using their influence to help hold back humanistic innovations, programs, and curriculum in their classrooms.

Unfortunately, other Christian teachers have unwittingly accepted, espoused, and even defended humanistic education, apparently never realizing that the educational philosophy they embrace is in severe contradiction to the Christianity they profess.

Some Christian teachers are having to make hard decisions. In 1974 one young teacher chose not to renew her contract with a public school for reasons of conscience, and took a $2,000 cut in annual pay to teach at a private school.

This points to the need for Christian teachers employed by public schools to band together for their job security, as well as for the spiritual and intellectual welfare of children in their charge.

Because of their position, statements by teachers are more likely to be accepted and acted upon by school boards, than are the same statements made by "unqualified" parents about the same textbooks or films. Visualize the potential effectiveness of Christian school teachers going as a group before school boards and voicing their objection to a series of books, or a film or methodology in use in their district. Suppose their objection rests on the grounds that the particular film or textbook promotes the tenets of a nontheistic religion and therefore violates the "establishment of religion" clause of the First Amendment. Would school board members dare ignore their request to remove such materials?

Teachers have been quite successful through organized efforts in recent years, in gaining teacher benefits. Can they not muster similar strength and effectiveness in behalf of a generation of American children?

There are enough teachers in the public schools of America who call themselves evangelical Christians to literally turn the tide for good — if, as a group, they would put their shoulder to the wheel.

(4) State legislators are in a privileged position to take positive action to protect the Constitutional religious rights of Christian children and their parents. They can introduce and work for legislation which forbids the use of textbooks, curriculum, or methodology that promotes agnosticism, atheism, or the religion of Secular Humanism. Laws are needed that provide stiff penalties for teachers found guilty of using such materials or promoting such philosophies in public schools. Such laws should be written in a manner to protect students from lopsided presentations concerning the origin of the earth and man. Laws are also needed which provide penalties for teaching rebellion against authority to children in public schools.

It is not enough to have positive laws on the books which state the schools shall teach patriotism and respect for authority and provide "basic education." Providing penalties for offensive teaching and invasion-of-privacy through testing, would be a protective measure, and give parents ground to stand on.

Constant vigilance should be exercised at state level (as well as in Washington), to protect children from the potential tyranny of social engineering via PPBS machinery. Passing legislation which forbids testing or record-keeping in the affective (values, beliefs, attitudes) domain would offer some protection in this direction.

(5) Senators and representatives in Washington are in a position to offer great assistance in salvaging public education.

An article entitled "Hiding Behind Noble Purpose, Education Office Squanders Tax Money," appeared in an Oregon newspaper in 1972. "Millions for 'lemons,' and this is just a sample," said the lead line. The article was written by Edith Green, (a former school teacher), who at that time was serving as a Representative to Congress from Oregon. Her comments followed a two-year study of contracts and grants awarded by the United States Office of Education. Examples of "bad management and useless educational projects" were cited. [2]

As bad as squandering millions for worthless projects may be, even worse is spending taxpayers' money for education which undermines parental beliefs.

When legislators in Washington appropriate millions of dollars for federal aid to education, they may be making a major contribution to the problems of public education rather than to solutions. They could, I believe, take a giant stride toward the goal of salvaging public education by simply cutting all federal aid forthwith and by reducing federal income tax correspondingly. Consider the tremendous waste of money spent on programs of questionable value. Consider the potential damage to children subjected to programs such as P.A.C.E., [3] the Title III project for experimental education.

The matter of grants dished out by federal agencies must also be reckoned with.

Dr. Onalee S. McGraw (Ph.D. in government) has urged senators and representatives to:

Introduce or support legislation setting forth strict guidelines, enforced by legislative oversight, to insure that grants given for educational purposes

(a) require philosophical and political neutrality

(b) do not violate the sanctity of the home and the privacy of the child, and

(c) preclude the manipulation of teachers and students through the selective presentation of content and psychological "behavior management" techniques. [4]

Such legislation is urgently needed in view of tremendous grants which have been channelled, for example, to certain university-based behavior "shapers." (One "shaper" alone was the recipient of almost a million dollars in grants, according to a writer in the November, 1972, issue of *Psychology Today*.)

The social studies program, M.A.C.O.S. is an example of a course which is highly objectionable on religious grounds to some parents. The

National Science Foundation supplied grants under which M.A.C.O.S. was developed.

And isn't it appalling that financial support by the U.S. Office of Education contributed to the development of such literature books as *Coping* and *Rebels and Regulars* (Macmillan Company, Gateway English series)? Some parents find these books extremely offensive and disgusting.

Can the use of tax dollars dispensed through federal agencies, for education that undermines or violates religious beliefs of children and their parents, be Constitutionally justified?

What About Private Schools?

Lecturer and journalist, Russell Kirk, believes ". . .every man of conscience ought to strive for purgation of our stumbling school system, encumbered as it is with silly impedimenta and baneful errors." [5] I agree. Certainly every person in the groups named, as well as every parent, grandparent, and taxpayer, has an obligation to work for the restoration of genuine education and the elimination of anti-Christian propaganda in the public schools.

Any efforts to bring about such a restoration can be expected to meet with bitter resistance from certain factions. "Only if we understand clearly that the battle of education mirrors the large-scale war among clashing philosophies do we have a better chance of sizing up the issues and controversies correctly." [6] The war is, in the final analysis, a religious war. Those of the humanistic persuasions of John Dewey, whose philosophy has so long dominated public education, cannot be expected to turn loose easily or quickly. Such changes sometimes take years. In the meantime, a generation of Christian children must be saved from indoctrination in socialistic and humanistic beliefs.

The need for private schools, therefore, is urgent and immediate.

Space does not permit a lengthy discussion on how to open and operate a private school; other books are available on this subject. We can consider only a few points here.

The first and most important point I can make is that private schools should not be carbon copies of the present public schools. There is no reason why they should not be academically superior to public schools. They can provide a vastly improved moral atmosphere.

Cost is a necessary concern. Many taxpayers and parents have become increasingly aware in recent years that financial input does not necessarily guarantee intellectual output. They have watched the Sacred Cow, public education, gobble up more and more of the green stuff, while the product has not seemed to improve. Spending and learning are not necessarily synonymous.

Children can learn in a modest environment. A building that is clean and warm, and meets fire and safety regulations and sanitary standards should prove quite adequate for a private school.

Virtually all children, regardless of their academic ability or IQ, are still required to take twelve years to complete the work necessary to get their high school diploma. Perhaps as many as one-fourth, or even more, could cover the material in nine or ten years. Why should they be held back to finish with the slowest? Permitting those who are competent to move ahead, to obtain their diplomas in less time, is another money-saving possibility.

Many persons pay prohibitive property taxes, the lion's share of which, in at least some states, goes to public education. Many of these persons also voluntarily and regularly pay ten per cent of their income (some far more) to the churches of their choice. This is true even in lower income tax brackets. Why? They believe in that which they are supporting. Could we not assume that many would likewise voluntarily support education in private schools, if those schools were in agreement with their religious beliefs, and if they had confidence those schools were doing a good job academically? And particularly if the back-breaking tax burden was drastically reduced?

Persons who are financially able should consider making scholarships available to private schools of their choice. This would enable some children to attend whose parents are financially unable to pay even very moderate tuition.

Another factor should not be overlooked: Many Christian teachers might welcome the opportunity to teach for less pay in a private school where curriculum, discipline, and dress codes are more in keeping with their own religious convictions.

Time, like money, can be misspent. Shortening the length of the school day to three hours in the first three grades, is another way money could be saved. This would reduce teacher salary expenditures. The main emphasis in the first three grades should be upon competent mastery of the basic skills: reading, writing, and arithmetic. The learning potential for subject matter in later years should be greatly increased through mastery of these skills in the lower grades. Future expense of "remedial reading" and "Special Education" teacher salaries can thereby be greatly reduced, if not totally avoided.

The importance of correct spelling should be emphasized as soon as children begin to write whole words. When children begin writing whole sentences and short compositions, correct grammar and punctuation should be taught. (This will avoid the necessity of unlearning and relearning later.)

As the child's reading proficiency and vocabulary increase, interesting nonfiction books as well as worth-while story books can be introduced. Look-say-nothing books should be avoided.

By the end of the third grade, most children should be able to read books on various subjects quite proficiently, write legibly, demonstrate accuracy in grammatical usage, and spell accurately, at their grade level. They should also have a good understanding of the meaning and purpose of numbers and of the processes of addition, subtraction, multiplication, and simple division.

Beginning in the fourth grade, the school day could be lengthened to five or six hours.

"Geography of the United States and the world should be taught as separate, logically organized subjects in the fourth and sixth grades, in that order. . . . United States history should be taught in chronological order in the fifth grade." [7]

Common sense dictates desks should be placed in straight rows all facing one direction — toward the teacher. With the now-popular circles and other variations, physical movement and eye-to-eye contact with other children are distractive to the learning process.

Correspondence courses are now being used in some small private schools. These may work quite well where schools are set up on the basis of the old one-room country school, where there are several grades in one room, or no students at all in some grades. They also offer an alternative to parents who are energetic enough to teach their own children at home, in areas where no private schools exist, and where state laws permit. (Perhaps it is time to challenge, in court, those state laws which forbid parental teaching in the home.)

Criticism levelled at parents who consider teaching their children at home frequently goes something like this: "Oh, you shouldn't isolate those children." What are they being "isolated" from? Morbid, profane literature? Agnostic teaching? Sensitivity training? UN propaganda? Indoctrination in the religion of evolution? A V.D.-infected crowd? Drug pushers?

Probably ninety-five out of every one hundred American children live in neighborhoods where there are other children with whom they can "socialize" two or three hours a day.

Tax Credits and Vouchers

In June, 1973, the United States Supreme Court banned indirect aid by the states through either tax credits or tuition payments to parents whose children attend parochial schools. They also banned direct reimbursement for maintenance and testing. It is believed this action may close the door to both tax credit possibilities and the use of vouchers at the federal as well as at state level. Even so, both tax credits and the voucher system warrant discussion.

More than twenty bills were introduced in Congress in early 1973 which would have authorized an income tax credit for a portion of the tuition paid by parents whose children attend private or parochial schools.

Why should any parent who is paying the entire cost of his children's education in a private school, be required to pay the same amount of taxes — property taxes and otherwise — as if his children were in the public schools? In many cases, this constitutes a double injustice: Such parents are financially discriminated against by having to bear an unfair share of the cost of education. Furthermore, some of their tax dollars may be spent for propagation of ideas detrimental to their religious beliefs.

A voucher system, some believe, is a possible answer. Under this plan, parents would be given a voucher to be presented to the school of the parents' choice. The voucher could be cashed (from tax funds) by the school. Parents could enroll their children in public schools, in existing private schools, or could join with others of like views and establish their own new private schools.

A voucher system should upgrade the quality of education through competition; it should help end religious discrimination against those who choose private, church-related schools. It should help to break the grip of the relativist-socialist-leaning thought-form that permeates so much of the public system.

But a voucher system would be desirable only under the condition that private schools accepting them would remain free of government control. For should private schools ever fall under the control and manipulation of the state, we would be far worse off than now. This we know:

"There is no hope left for individual freedom in this or any other country, if the Statist octopus is allowed to also swallow the private and parochial schools." [8]

'An Immoral Premise"

Furthermore, even with a tax-supported voucher system, completely free of government manipulation, were that possible, our schools would still be operating financially on a socialist concept. Socialism forces one to contribute from his financial resources to pay for the benefit of another. In *Education in America,* George Charles Roche III asks:

Why should the money of one citizen be taken by force to finance the education of other peoples' children, any more than to finance the building of other peoples' homes, the gasoline for other peoples' cars, the payment of other peoples' medical expenses? I have yet to hear a compelling *moral* argument justifying coercion for such a purpose.

So long as we are willing to allow an immoral premise to dominate our educational endeavors, we must be willing to live with ugly results. The only lasting solution is to remove education from the hands of government, restoring responsibility to the student and to the parent.

The response at that point tends to be, "Why, if there were no public education, parents wouldn't send their children to school!" I have yet to meet the person who will not send *his* children to school. It is always those *other people* who would supposedly be remiss in their duty. [9]

In this regard, it is interesting to note the compulsory education law was repealed in Mississippi in 1956. A state department of education official has said no significant change occurred in the dropout rate at the time the law was repealed.

The Cupertino Story

Even though public school financing (through involuntary taxation) and compulsory school attendance laws are acknowledged to be totalitarian concepts, both are existent realities. Neither is likely to disappear tomorrow or next year. Parents who do not live near private schools compatible with their religious beliefs, or who cannot financially meet the expense of private education, should give serious thought to another possibility.

An encouraging story of a project in Cupertino, California, is told in the May, 1974, *Bulletin* of the Council for Basic Education (CBE). Cupertino is a large district which serves 21,000 students (kindergarten through eighth grade). The *Bulletin* reports innovations recently promoted in the district have included: "student contracts, activity centers, individualized instruction, team teaching, differentiated staffing, open classes, and optional report cards. District philosophy is aimed at development of the 'whole child,' education is 'child-centered,' and the latest notions of author-critic-psychologists have been making steady inroads into the teaching process. . . ." [10]

In May, 1973, seven parents requested the school board consider granting an alternative to the innovations. They wanted a program "aimed toward providing strong emphasis on basic skills, rote and drill, the Golden Rule, friendly competition, reasonable code of dress and deportment, teacher-directed instruction, teacher-class discussion of subject matter, continuity of curriculum, standardized testing, letter-graded report cards, and self-contained classrooms sans [without] aids or volunteers. And no contract learning except in enrichment areas!" [11]

By September, the list of applicants for the new program had grown from an initial 400 "to over a thousand children." [12] The board gave them the green light; however, due to limitations of space and staff, they were able to accommodate only 160 of the applicants. These students were placed "in one school, grades one through six. Transportation for students from outside that school area is provided by parents." [13]

Education — Whose Responsibility?

Many of us have come to believe the only way to become educated is by attending school (especially public school) five or six hours a day, nine months a year, twelve or more years.

Have we forgotten some of our most brilliant and outstanding forebears had very little formal schooling?

How many of today's Ph.D.s could match the intellectual genius, the versatility, the statesmanship of Benjamin Franklin? He, with two years of formal schooling, was presented doctorates by two universities in England and honored by kings and statesmen in Europe.[14]

How many of today's learned, possess the gentle wisdom, humility, and eloquence of Abraham Lincoln, whose formal schooling totalled less than one year?

And where would we be today without the thousand inventions of a man whose classroom instruction totalled three months — Thomas Alva Edison?

A number of living examples could be cited among well-known personalities, who are financially prosperous and highly successful in various fields, from entertainers to business magnates, who were public school dropouts. Such examples raise important questions.

As long as the child's education leaves him academically proficient and morally upright (how well does public education score here?), what right does the state have to dictate *where* and *how* that education occurs? Who holds the final jurisdiction over the child — the *parents* or the *state?* In a pluralistic, free society, the decisions of where and how the child is educated should rest with the parents alone.

> The pursuit of education, like the pursuit of happiness, is an individual affair. It can start with parents, but it ends with oneself. The state has no logical role to play in it except to provide the conditions of freedom in which individuals can work out their own destinies in their own way.
>
> Ideally, in our free society, government should be . . . uninvolved with education. . . ."[15]

Such ideas come as a shock to many of us who have been brainwashed all our lives to accept totalitarian concepts of education.

"God, in His Divine Wisdom and Providence ordained that children should be placed in the guardianship of parents. Because God, not the state, has granted these particular parents the privilege of guardianship over these particular children, parents are ultimately responsible to God for the training and education of their children."[16]

Now is the time to assert the truth that education is the respon-

sibility of parents. Now is the time to establish legislative safe-
guards of that parental responsibility. . . . Because tax-supported education is committed to religious views that are
contrary to the Judeo-Christian traditions, it is time for all who
hold such traditions to claim the protection of the Constitution.[17]

Why should tax-supported schools be used to further humanistic
education any more than Mormon education or Catholic education or
Baptist education? Why should Humanists not "set up their own
'religious' schools"?[18]

Our imperatives now come into sharp focus: If public schools are to be
permitted to survive, they must be re-routed from their present direction.
In the meantime, Christian parents who care about their children should
remove them from the influence of humanistic education, and place
them in private schools wherever satisfactory private schools exist, or
where new ones can be established.

NOTES

1 L.H. Dale, "Sensible Woman," (Portland) *Oregonian*, December 19,
1970.

2 Edith Green, "Millions for 'lemons,' and This is Just a Sample: Hiding
Behind Noble Purpose, Education Office Squanders Tax Money," (Portland)
Sunday Oregonian, August 6, 1972, p. F3.

3 Projects to Advance Creativity in Education (also sometimes referred to as
Planning to Accelerate Change in Education); made possible by Elementary and
Secondary Education Act (ESEA) of Congress, 1965. Title III of that Act
encouraged use of innovations; federal funds were made available for experimentation.

4 Onalee S. McGraw, "If More Parents Only Knew: What Educators Are
Doing With Your Federal Taxes," *Human Events*, August 14, 1971, p. 625/17.

5 Russell Kirk, Foreword to *The Future of Education* by Thomas Molnar,
Revised Edition (New York City: Fleet Academic Editions, Inc., Copyright 1961,
1970), p. 17.

6 Thomas Molnar, *The Future of Education*, Revised Edition (New York
City: Fleet Academic Editions, Inc.; Copyright 1961, 1970), p. 23.

7 Carl F. Hansen, *Emphasis on Basic Education at the Amidon Elementary
School*, Occasional Papers Number One (Washington, D.C.: Council for Basic

Education, November, 1961; June, 1962; January, 1964); p. 10; originally delivered as an address to the annual meeting of the Council for Basic Education in Washington on October 7, 1961. Parts of the pamphlet are included in Dr. Hansen's book, *The Amidon Elementary School: A Successful Demonstration in Basic Education,* (Englewood Cliffs, N.J.: Prentice-Hall, Inc., 1962).

8 Deloris Feak, "A Look at the Full Scope of the New Education," mimeographed paper (an address prepared for a World History class at Saratoga Campus, West Valley College, Saratoga, California, June, 1972), p. 7.

9 George Charles Roche III, *Education in America* (Irvington-on-Hudson, New York: Foundation for Economic Education, Inc.; ©1969 by George Charles Roche III), pp. 153, 154.

10 Mrs. Harrell Bell, "Basic Education in Cupertino," *Bulletin,* Council for Basic Education, Vol. 18, No. 9, May, 1974, p. 14.

11 *Ibid.,* p. 15.

12 *Ibid.*

13 *Ibid.*

14 *Encyclopaedia Brittanica,* 1949, s.v. "Benjamin Franklin."

15 Samuel L. Blumenfeld, *How to Start Your Own Private School — and Why You Need One* (New Rochelle, New York: Arlington House, 1972), p. 344.

16 Opal Moore, paper presented to House Education Committee on House Bill 2978, Salem, Oregon, April 10, 1973, p. 6.

17 John F. Blanchard, Jr., *Myths of Public Education,* pamphlet (Wheaton, Illinois: National Association of Christian Schools; reprinted from the *Good News Broadcaster;* ©1972 by the Good News Broadcasting Association, Inc.).

18 "Whose Morals Do You Use in a Morality Code?" United Parents Under God, Box 593, Belmont, California.

20

A CHALLENGE THAT MUST BE MET

Let history talk to you! Every great reform, every grand inspiring movement in the world's history has grown from the defiant stand of determined will against surrounding forces.

... C. M. Ward

It has been said a problem is half-solved when it has been acknowledged and well-defined. A thorough understanding alone will not solve the problem. Action must follow understanding. "Faith without works is dead." [1]

Those who are in positions to help bring restoration to public education can begin immediately to strive toward that goal. While efforts are being made in that direction, establishment of multitudes of new independent schools is imperative. It is time for evangelical churches to assume their long-neglected duty of training their young. H. Edward Rowe declares:

> Thousands of new Christian schools must be established — and they must be Christian not only in doctrine but in practice. They must include in the curriculum all dimensions of Christian application on all of the issues of our day. Only in this way will they produce a generation of mature, well-balanced Christians . . . who will be able to provide the necessary leadership in the coming generation. [2] It will not do to practice secular educational techniques under the roof of a school that is called "Christian." [3]

The curriculum, textbook content, and methodology in Christian schools must reflect the Christian philosophy. Textbooks to help fill such needs are now being written by qualified Christian scholars and educators.

Many churches already have beautiful buildings sitting idle all week that could serve as day school facilities, where parents could have their children educated in accord with their religious beliefs.

The particular issues involved in setting up private schools will vary from state to state because of differences in state laws. Even restrictive state laws should not be seen as ironclad, immovable gates. They, too, can be changed with persistent, determined effort.

The value of trustworthy legal advice should never be overlooked.

The National Association of Christian Schools (NACS) exists for the purpose of assisting in the organization of new Christian schools and strengthening existing ones. They offer numerous publications, curriculum guides, cassettes, and a "New School Starter Kit."

A few good books are available which should prove helpful. One of these is Samuel L. Blumenfeld's *How to Start Your Own Private School — And Why You Need One* (Arlington House). Another is *How to Start Your Own School* (Macmillan) by Robert Love. Ask your library for others.

Constant vigilance at legislative levels must be exercised to protect existing and future private schools. In states where crippling laws are already on the books, blueprints for dismantling such statutes should be drawn and pursued. Dismantling, in some cases, might be accomplished through legislation or with test cases in court.

Remember, it is only a comparative handful who write laws for the rest of us. Legislators are extremely busy persons. Public education lobbies are powerful. Legislators may act in good faith and still pass unfortunate laws, simply because they have heard only one side of an issue. Make certain your side is heard in your state. When legislators take the oath to uphold the United States Constitution, they have an obligation to protect and defend the Constitutional rights of religious minorities.

As independent schools, particularly Christian schools, multiply and flourish, it is almost inevitable that pressure will rapidly come to bear on legislators to bring private schools under tighter jurisdiction of state boards of education.

A few months after the Boohers won their case in court in Oregon to teach their own daughter, a foot-in-the-door draft for a bill was considered by a State Senate Interim Education Committee. The bill would have established "licensing procedures for private schools." It would also have provided (as a condition for licensing) that: "The curriculum in grades 1 through 12" would be "substantially similar to the courses of study usually taught in these grades in the public schools for a period of time equivalent to that required for children attending public schools."

Such a provision speaks precisely of the kind of curricular conformity many adherents of private education wish to avoid.

The proposal to license private schools in Oregon was strongly favored by the State Public School Superintendent. He was concerned because anyone could "hang out a shingle" [4] and start a private school. Seeing no "current and present danger," [5] the committee tabled the bill.

That Fall (1972) numerous private schools opened in the Portland area. As might be expected, another attempt was made at licensing private schools during the next session of the legislature in 1973. The bill (verbatim in part to the one tabled by the Senate Interim Committee) was considered this time by the House Committee on Education. At a public hearing, qualified persons spoke convincingly against the bill, and it was tabled.

These cases demonstrate that proponents of private schools must be alert. They must be prepared to move swiftly. They must speak convincingly of the value of pluralistic education.

They should have at hand accurate information and statistics on both private and public schools. Results of studies of academic proficiency of students in private schools compared to proficiency of students in public schools could be presented.

Multiplying the number of children attending private schools in your state, times the cost-per-year-per-child in public schools will give you an idea of how many millions of dollars private schools are saving taxpayers in your state. Legislators should be reminded of this savings to taxpayers.

It should be respectfully called to the attention of legislators that it is their duty to fortify "the rights of parents who believe that the 'free exercise of religion,' as guaranteed by the First Amendment, requires that they [the parents] provide an education for their children that is consistent with their religious faith. . . . If it is constitutional to be a Christian in the United States, the constitutional protection of the rights of education that is Christian must be observed by the state. . . ." [6]

Legislators are often sensitive to public sentiment, particularly as it affects their stand on a particular issue. For that reason, letters to the editor of your local newspaper may be effective, in that they help inform others. Such letters should be factual, short, persuasive, and always defensible.

A good time to write or talk to legislators is between sessions, when they are less rushed.

In addition to writing letters to legislators, appear personally at legislative hearings on pertinent bills, whenever possible. Look your best, and always be courteous. Be prepared to speak concisely and forcefully. Better five minutes of effective speaking than thirty minutes of droning. Never make a statement you cannot document and explain. If possible, have your remarks typewritten, double-spaced, and leave copies with the committee. (This will enable them to later review what you have said.)

Failure to act at crucial times by those who have worked diligently setting up private schools may result in their efforts being nullified by powers in high places.

Along with whatever human effort you put forth — whether at the legislative level, or in helping establish an independent school, or in working to free public schools from the influence of Secular Humanism — learn to draw from Strength and Knowledge and Wisdom greater than your own. Let prayer undergird every effort you make.

If you do not know the Risen Christ, ask Him, in your own words, to forgive your sins and to direct your paths. Commit your total self to God and ask Him to use your life for His honor. Begin to read your Bible. Thank God every day for the blessings of living in America. Each day ask Him to show you what He would have you to do *today*.

God can use ordinary people — unlikely people — to do great and mighty works for Him.

God chose an inarticulate Moses to stand before a stubborn Pharoah in behalf of his people. And the day came when that same humble Moses led a nation out of slavery.

A mighty army was set to flight by a little band of three hundred under the leadership of a modest farmer named Gideon — whom God had placed in charge.

A ruddy shepherd lad, armed only with a sling and a few pebbles, slew the might scoffing Goliath and brought victory to his people.

Down through the ages God has had His Ruths and Naomis, His Esthers; His Noahs, Daniels, and Jeremiahs; His Luthers, Wesleys, and Spurgeons.

Down through the ages they have "through faith subdued kingdoms, wrought righteousness, obtained promises, stopped the mouths of lions, quenched the violence of fire, escaped the edge of the sword, out of weakness were made strong, waxed valiant in fight, turned to flight the armies of the aliens." [7]

How were these feats accomplished? Through faith. Faith in themselves? No. Through faith in God.

And God has His witnesses among us today — the salt of the earth — men and women who are battling principalities and powers of darkness in high places for your children and mine. A few of them have been quoted in the pages of this book. Others' names you will never hear. They are part of the growing force of ordinary people who are standing in the gap where they are. They include those who are saying quietly, but determinedly, "We have had enough of humanistic public education. Let's save our children. Let's start our own private school." And they are doing it.

And as these forces grow, and as new Christian schools multiply, a new element, a power for good will become evident. These will not be children of darkness, floundering in the uncertain quagmire of agnosticism, or groping in the gray fog of relativism.

Rather they will display hope and courage and faith in God. Because they will respect and obey God's laws, their bodies will not be ravaged by venereal disease, alcohol, and drugs; their minds will be alert and clear. Intellectually and academically competent, and morally upright, they will comprise a beautiful new elite, capable of the kind of leadership for tomorrow that this nation, even today, so direly needs.

> The future has never been shaped by majorities but rather by dedicated minorities. And free men do not wait for the future; they create it. The difficulties and problems in that venture are to them not a hindrance but a challenge that must be met. [8]

The need for private schools was never greater. The challenge was never greater. The opportunities were never greater.

"We must remind ourselves, as courageous men of past ages have done, that the results are in the hands of God, but the duties are ours. It is time we met them." [9]

The children you save may be your own.

NOTES

1 James 2:26b.

2 H. Edward Rowe, "Christians Have a Job to Do," *Applied Christianity*, Vol. 2, No. 2, February, 1973, p. 28.

3 *Ibid.*

4 Robert Shepard, "Education Statement to Provide Guidelines," (UPI), *Roseburg* (Ore.) *News-Review*, September 13, 1972.

5 *Ibid.*

6 John F. Blanchard, Jr., *Myths of Public Education*, pamphlet (Wheaton, Illinois: National Association of Christian Schools, by permission of Good News Broadcaster; ©1972 by Good News Broadcasting Association, Inc.).

7 Heb. 11:33, 34.

8 Rousas John Rushdoony, *The Messianic Character of American Education*, paperback (Nutley, New Jersey: The Craig Press, 1968; ©1963), p. 332.

9 Rousas John Rushdoony, *Chalcedon Report* No. 94, June, 1973, p. 3.

ACKNOWLEDGEMENTS OF EPIGRAM SOURCES

Chapter
1. "Are Your Children Being Taught 'To Think'?"
   Francis A. Schaeffer, *The God Who Is There*, paperback ed., ©1968 (Third American printing, Downers Grove, Ill.: Inter-Varsity Press, December, 1969, with permission from Hodder and Stoughton Limited, England), p. 140. (hereafter cited as Francis A. Schaeffer, *The God Who Is There*).
2. "The Uncertain World of the Gray Thinkers"
   Billy Graham, "What the Bible Says to Me," *Reader's Digest*, Vol. 94, No. 565; May, 1969, pp. 85, 86.
3. "Look Who's Widening the Generation Gap"
   Francis A. Schaeffer, *The God Who Is There*, p. 13.
4. "The Importance of Memory"
   Richard M. Weaver, *Visions of Order: The Cultural Crisis of Our Time*, paperback ed., (Baton Rouge: Louisiana State University Press, 1964; manufactured in the United States by Vail-Ballou Press, Inc., Binghamton, N.Y.), p. 49.
5. "Quack Psychologists in the Classroom"
   Joseph P. Bean, M.D., *Public Education: River of Pollution*, (text of public speech made at Glendale, California, announcing Dr. Bean's resignation from Glendale Board of Education), n.d. (Fullerton, California: Educator Publications), p. 18.
6. "Teaching Children 'To Cope' With Life"
   C.M. Ward, Revivaltime Radio Sermon, "Bound," April 18, 1971.
7. "How Scientific is the Theory of Evolution?"
   Edwin Conklin quoted by Louis Cassels, UPI, "Challenge of the '70's: Man Must Find A Reason For Own Existence," *The News-Review*, (Roseburg, Oregon), December 10, 1969.
8. "Prescriptions for Social Problems"
   Rousas J. Rushdoony, *The Messianic Character of American Education* (Nutley, N.J.: The Craig Press 1968, ©1963), p. 230.
9. "Let's Analyze Reading Programs — Not Children"
   Charles H. Brower, *The Return of the Square*, pamphlet, (printed and distributed by America's Future, Inc., New Rochelle, New York; ©1962, Batten, Barton, Durstine & Osborn, Inc., New

York), p. 4.

10. "Social Studies for Social Change"
    Albert Lynd, *Quackery in the Public Schools,* paperback ed., (New York: Grosset & Dunlap, *Grosset's* Universal *Library* by arrangement with Little, Brown and Company; ©1950, 1953 by Albert Lynd), p. 53.

11. "The New English — A Revolt Against Rigid Rules"
    Arthur Bestor, "School Crisis, U.S.A.: Getting Away With Mistakes in English," *Good Housekeeping,* August, 1958, p. 221.

12. "Modern Literature — Avenue to Culture or Corruption?"
    James Allen, *As A Man Thinketh,* (Fleming H. Revell Company, n.d., n.p.), p. 31.

13. "Is the New Math a Big Mistake?"
    T. Robert Ingram, "The New Math and Twisted Minds," mimeographed article, n.d. (distributed by The Mel Gablers, P.O. Box 7175, Longview, Texas).

14 "Sex Education for the Now Generation"
    Jenkin Lloyd Jones, *Who is Tampering With the Soul of America?,* pamphlet (reprinted as a public service by America's Future, Inc., New Rochelle, N.Y.), p. 1.

15 "PPBS — Their Program is to Program"
    Thomas Jefferson.

16. "The Equality Myth"
    Curtis B. Dall, *F.D.R.: My Exploited Father-in-Law,* paperback, Second Edition, (Tulsa, Oklahoma: Christian Crusade Publications, ©1968), p. 58.

17. "School Prayers and Religious Discrimination"
    Nicholas Wolterstorff, *Religion and the Schools,* A Reformed Journal Monograph, (Grand Rapids, Michigan: William B. Eerdmans Publishing Co.; ©1965, 1966 by Wm. B. Eerdmans Publishing Co. This material, in slightly different form, first appeared in the *Reformed Journal*), p. 36.

18. "A State Church in Disguise"
    Mrs. Basil [Ruth] Denison, "State Church," *Roseburg* (Ore.) *News-Review,* June 24, 1971.

19. "A Look at Alternatives"
    George W. Seevers, "Freedom of Worship — Humbug!", mimeo-

graphed paper, n.d., p. 3.
20. "A Challenge That Must Be Met"
C.M. Ward, Revivaltime Radio Sermon, "Environment,"
March 21, 1971.

SUGGESTED FURTHER READING

Beyond Freedom and Dignity, B.F. Skinner (New York, New York: Alfred A. Knopf, Inc., 1971).

The Branded Child, Edward J. Van Allen (New York, New York: Reportorial Press, 1964).

Christianity and Civilisation, Volumes I and II, Emil Brunner (New York: Charles Scribner's Sons, 1948, 1949).

The Christian School: Why It is Right for Your Child, Paul A. Kienel (Wheaton, Illinois: Victor Books, Division of SP Publications, Inc., 1974).

A Common Faith, John Dewey (New Haven: Yale University Press, 1934).

Competent to Counsel, Jay E. Adams (Nutley, New Jersey: Presbyterian and Reformed Publishing Company, Box 185, 1973).

A Consumer's Guide to Educational Innovations, Mortimer Smith, Richard Peck, and George Weber (Washington, D.C.: Council for Basic Education, 1972).

Education in America, George Charles Roche III (Irvington-on-Hudson, New York: Foundation for Economic Education, Inc., 1969).

The Future of Education, Thomas Molnar (New York City: Fleet Academic Editions, Inc., 1970).

The God Who is There, Francis A. Schaeffer (Downers Grove, Illinois: Inter-Varsity Press 1968).

The Great Deceit: Social Pseudo-Sciences, A Veritas Foundation Staff Study; Zymund Dobbs, Research Director (West Sayville, New York: Veritas Foundation, 1964).

Have the Public Schools "Had It"? Elmer L. Towns (Nashville/New York: Thomas Nelson Inc., 1974).

How to Start Your Own Private School — and Why You Need One, Samuel L. Blumenfeld (New Rochelle, New York: Arlington House, 1972).

Intellectual Schizophrenia: Culture, Crisis and Education. Rousas J. Rushdoony (Philadelphia: Presbyterian and Reformed Publishing Company, 1971).

The Messianic Character of American Education, Rousas J. Rushdoony (Nutley, New Jersey: The Craig Press, 1968).

Moral Philosophy, Jacques Maritain (New York: Charles Scribner's Sons, 1964).

The Mythology of Science, Rousas J. Rushdoony (Nutley, New Jersey: The Craig Press, 1967).

The Philosophy of Humanism, Corliss Lamont (New York: Frederick Ungar Publishing Company, 1965).

Poison Drops in the Federal Senate, Zach. Montgomery (Washington. Gibson Bros., 1886; available from St. Thomas Press, P.O. Box 35096, Houston, Texas).

Reading Without Dick and Jane, Arther S. Trace, Jr. (Chicago: Henry Regnery Company, 1965).

The Remarkable Birth of Planet Earth, Henry M. Morris (San Diego: Institute for Creation Research, 1972).

The Sanctity of Sex, Revised Edition, Olford and Lawes (Old Tappan, New Jersey: Fleming H. Revell Company, 1963).

Teaching as a Subversive Activity, Neil Postman and Charles Weingartner (New York: Delacorte Press, 1969)

Tomorrow's Illiterates: The State of Reading Instruction Today, Charles C. Walcutt, editor (Boston-Toronto: Atlantic Monthly Press published by Little, Brown and Company, 1961).

Trousered Apes, Duncan Williams (New Rochelle, New York: Arlington House, 1972).

The Twilight of Evolution, Henry M. Morris (Grand Rapids, Michigan: Baker Book House, 1963).

Visions of Order: The Cultural Crisis of Our Time, Richard M. Weaver (Baton Rouge: Louisiana State University Press, 1964).

We Live by Faith, Ruby Lornell (Philadelphia: Muhlenberg Press, 1955).

Why Johnny Can't Read, Rudolf Flesch (New York: Harper & Row, Publishers, 1955).

BOOKLETS, PAMPHLETS, ARTICLES

"Are Public Schools Religious Seminaries?" *The Barbara M. Morris Report* (P.O.Box 412, Ellicott City, Maryland), Vol. 5, No. 3, June, 1974.

Back to Freedom and Dignity, Francis A. Schaeffer (Downers Grove, Illinois: Inter-Varsity Press, 1972).

'The Case Against Religion," Albert Ellis (New York, New York: Institute for Rational Living, Inc., 45 East 65th Street).

The Dilemma of Education, Cornelius Van Til (Presbyterian and Reformed Publishing Company, 1956).

The Elementary Schools (New Canaan, Connecticut: The Long House Publishers, Inc., P.O. Box 3).

"Forecast for the '70's," Harold G. Shane and June Grant Shane, *Today's Education — NEA Journal,* January 1969.

"Freedom of Worship — Humbug!" George W. Seevers (Tampa, Florida: 701 East Caracas).

Love, Courtship, and Marriage for Christian Youth, William W. Orr (Wheaton, Illinois: Scripture Press Publications, Inc.).

Humanist Manifesto II (San Francisco: American Humanist Association 125 El Camino del Mar).

Problems of Evolution, Stewart Custer (Greenville, South Carolina: Bob Jones University Press, 1964).

The Psychiatry of Enduring Peace and Social Progress, The William Alanson White Memorial Lectures, Second Series, G.B. Chisholm (Washington, D.C.: The William Alanson White Psychiatric Foundation, Inc.: reprinted from *Psychiatry,* Vol. 9, No. 1, February, 1946).

Public Education: River of Pollution, Joseph P. Bean, M.D. (Fullerton, California: Educator Publications, 1110 South Pomona Avenue).

Religion and the Schools, Nicholas Wolterstorff (Grand Rapids, Michigan: William B. Eerdmans Publishing Company, 1966).

Schools: Government or Public? T. Robert Ingram (Houston, Texas: St. Thomas Press, P.O. Box 35096, 1962).

Should Evolution Be Taught? John N. Moore (East Lansing, Michigan: P.O. Box 489, 1972).

So You Need A Psychologist? (*Psychology . . . Fact, Fiction or Fraud?*), B. Pollard (Los Angeles: Fundamental Evangelistic Association, P.O. Box 26157, 1972).

What's Happened to Our Schools? Rosalie M. Gordon (New Rochelle, New York: America's Future, Inc., 542 Main Street, 1965).

AUTHOR/TITLE INDEX

SUBJECT INDEX

IT'S GOO   **ger**
Introductic
The st   the
Billy Grah   y of
being a ra   ton,
D.C. May   an
emotionall   ople
was durin   arly
70's. Out o   ck's
raised cler   dis-
covered a
HARDCO   2.95

THE ABU
Introductic
The fir   use
by an auth   nts,
police auth   An
account of   xed
attitude tov   ixes
deal with   in
disciplinir   ins
16 pictures
HARDC   95

These   ng
directly fr

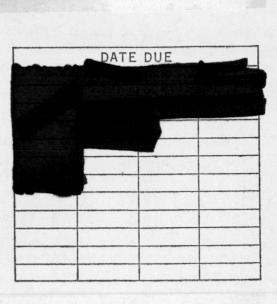